ALCOHOL PROBLEMS

A Report to the Nation
by the Cooperative Commission
on the Study of Alcoholism

PREPARED BY
THOMAS F. A. PLAUT

OXFORD UNIVERSITY PRESS
London   Oxford   New York

OXFORD UNIVERSITY PRESS

Oxford London New York
Glasgow Toronto Melbourne Wellington
Cape Town Salisbury Ibadan Nairobi Lusaka Addis Ababa
Bombay Calcutta Madras Karachi Lahore Dacca
Kuala Lumpur Hong Kong Tokyo

To
E. M. Jellinek

Preface

This document is the policy statement of the Cooperative Commission on the Study of Alcoholism.

The Cooperative Commission was established in 1961, financed by a grant from the National Institute of Mental Health (U.S. Department of Health, Education, and Welfare).[1] The original plan for the study was developed primarily by the North American Association of Alcoholism Programs, a United States and Canadian organization of governmental alcoholism programs. By agreement, the Cooperative Commission was created as a separate organization independent of the Association. The Commission membership was drawn from a variety of professions and scientific disciplines. Members were chosen to include some persons with professional experience in the field of alcohol problems and some from relevant disciplines irrespective of previous special interest in alcohol problems.

The Commission conducted a nationwide search for a

1. Thanks are expressed to the National Institute of Mental Health for this grant (#MH 09181), and to numerous members of its staff for invaluable assistance provided during the last six years.

scientific director and selected R. Nevitt Sanford. Dr. Sanford and the research staff[2] of the Commission established their offices at the Institute for the Study of Human Problems, Stanford University (California). The research activities have been conducted by Dr. Sanford and his associates. In addition, members of the Cooperative Commission have been directly and intimately involved in the work of the research staff.

This report, prepared by Thomas F. A. Plaut with the aid of other members of the research staff, is the product of the participation and considered judgment of the Commission members and carries their formal endorsement. Other publications by members of the staff will include a major volume entitled *Alcohol Problems and Public Policy* and several monographs on special aspects of alcohol problems. The volume *Alcohol Problems and Public Policy* will be a more theoretical and detailed treatment of many points and issues in this report.

The Cooperative Commission on the Study of Alcoholism anticipates that this report will be the basis for: (1) planned and coordinated action on recommendations dealing with a variety of alcohol problems, (2) widespread public discussions of many questions regarding alcohol use, (3) expanded training programs to provide needed personnel, and (4) vastly increased research to provide critically needed additional knowledge. This report and the publications to follow are initial efforts to achieve a better understanding of the totality of alcohol problems. Much needs to be done by the collaborative efforts of scientists, professional workers, legislators, government officials, individual citizens and many other organizations be-

2. See Appendix D for a list of members of the research staff.

fore the problems associated with alcohol use can be effectively dealt with.

Appreciation is expressed for many significant contributions, both as a senior staff member and as an active Commissioner, to the late Dr. E. M. Jellinek, to whom this report is respectfully and endearingly dedicated.

New York City   COOPERATIVE COMMISSION ON
October 1, 1966   THE STUDY OF ALCOHOLISM

Members of the Cooperative Commission on the Study of Alcoholism

H. David Archibald, *Chairman (Interim Commission) 1960-1961*
Executive Director
Alcoholism and Drug Addiction Research Foundation of Ontario
Toronto, Canada

Selden D. Bacon
Director
Rutgers Center of Alcohol Studies
Rutgers University
New Brunswick, New Jersey

Harold W. Demone
Executive Director
Medical Foundation, Inc.
Boston, Massachusetts

Ruth Fox, M.D.
Medical Director
National Council on Alcoholism, Inc.
New York, New York

Contents

1

Disagreement about alcohol use

1

Uses of alcohol

Beverage alcohol plays an important role in the lives of many Americans.[1] It is often considered essential for hospitality, and its use as a "social lubricant" is well known. Many American men have a drink with their noonday meal, and many men and women regularly drink at home in the evening. Leisure-time activities often include some drinking. Although most of these occasions do not present any difficulties, substantial disagreement and uncertainty may be found concerning drinking in America. For example, there is no consensus on how, if at all, teenagers should be prepared for participation in a society where most adults drink.

A sizeable minority of Americans[2] disapproves of any and all use of alcohol; in addition, even among users, there is

1. Approximately 70 per cent of adult Americans drink, and 40 per cent are regular drinkers (at least once a month). See H. A. Mulford, "Drinking and Deviant Drinking, U.S.A., 1963," *Quarterly Journal of Studies on Alcohol*, 25:634-50, 1964.
2. In this report the term "American" is used to include both the United States and Canada. Any reference to the United States alone will be indicated in the text.

substantial disagreement about what constitutes appropriate alcohol use and what is inappropriate use. Differing views are held about a number of alcohol questions, including drinking by youth, where and when alcoholic beverages should be sold, the impact of liquor advertising, the nature of alcoholism, and means of reducing alcohol-rated automobile accidents. Church groups still differ in their positions regarding the moral aspects of drinking. These are all "alcohol problems." The term "alcohol problem" as used in this report refers both to any controversy or disagreement about beverage alcohol use or non-use, and to any drinking behavior that is defined or experienced as a problem. Thus it includes both the difficulties that persons get into by drinking, and society's efforts to cope with these difficulties.

Alcoholism[3] is one major alcohol problem that has been receiving considerable attention. It causes suffering, endangers physical and emotional health, disrupts family relationships, and reduces economic effectiveness. The number of persons so affected by alcoholism and other kinds of problem drinking undoubtedly runs into the millions. In recent years physicians, social workers, clergymen, and other professional workers, as well as community leaders and government officials, have become more aware of the extent of these problems.

Although there has been an increased emphasis on alcoholism and other forms of problem drinking both by helping professions and agencies and also by the public, far less attention has been paid to broad issues in society regarding alcohol use and abuse. It is unlikely that substantial progress can be made with problem drinkers until the

3. See pp. 37-41 for definitions of the terms "alcoholism" and "problem drinking."

broader questions of alcohol use have been dealt with. Because these long-standing issues directly influence public and professional attitudes toward problem drinkers they are major factors impeding the development of needed treatment services.

2

Range of alcohol problems

Although alcoholism and other types of problem drinking are the major concern of health and medical workers, many groups and persons focus principally on very different alcohol problems. One such alcohol problem is the disagreement about what constitutes correct or appropriate drinking behavior. This confusion is apparent not only in the conflicting opinions expressed in statements by academic, legal, and other leaders, but is also evident among the general public. It is illustrated by the confused and often embarrassed reaction to persons intoxicated in public places. At a football game, for example, if a man is rather drunk, and some people in the crowd begin trying to control him or the police come to take him away, there are likely to be reactions from other spectators, including those not drinking. Some may resent the intrusion of the police; others will be less sympathetic to the man who is intoxicated; most spectators are glad they do not have to assume responsibility for doing something about the situation. The reactions of those persons seated close to the drunken man are often unpredictable, and may be pushed either in the direction of harshness or of tolerant amusement, depending on quite insignificant actions by the inebriated person or by one of the spectators. A lack of clearly defined standards about the use of alcoholic beverages can thus be seen in the uncertain reaction to drunkenness. Probably even more significant is the frequent joking about drinking. Expressions such as "sneak a quick one" or "have a blast" reveal uncertainty and mild guilt feelings which rarely accompany socially approved behavior.

At a different level are the possible difficulties of the host with his guests. In many parts of American society, serving drinks is a central element of hospitality. The host is expected to keep his guests' glasses full, even though a guest may drink too much and then behave objectionably. There is a reluctance, however, to interfere overtly in any way with a person's drinking except to offer him more! Seldom does a host tell a guest that he has had enough. It has been suggested that the host may have a responsibility to see to it that guests do not drink so much as to greatly increase the risk of automobile accidents when driving home. Currently, very few party-givers view this as part of their responsibility, but it does present a potential conflict. The host is supposed to see to it that his guests have a good time, but does this obligation entirely override that of protecting the safety and even the lives of the people he is entertaining, and the possible innocent victims of their dangerous driving?

Alcohol problems range from basic disagreement about the place of beverage alcohol in society, to those involving uses of alcohol that interfere with one's usual functioning, while still others concern disagreements over how to cope with unapproved drinking behavior. A basic cultural conflict is apparent in the varying conceptions of what constitutes the principal American alcohol problem. Physicians, public-health nurses, and welfare workers may consider alcoholism the central problem. In some communities, however, other alcohol-related problems, such as "driving under the influence," are seen as the major issue. Elsewhere, judging from newspaper stories, teenage drinking receives the most attention and particularly disturbs the adult community, associated as it often is with concern about sexual behavior and dangerous driving.

Public anxiety and frustration about major social issues such as racial unrest, automobile accidents, problems of urban living, and crime, lead to a search for simple explanations and solutions. Frequently alcohol is uncritically assumed to be the dominant cause of these and other social problems, and so set is this emotional response that on occasion alcohol is considered the major cause when subsequent investigation shows that it was entirely absent.

From the standpoint of prevention and education a serious difficulty has been created because disapproval of dangerous drinking has been confused with opposition to all drinking. Because most Americans now accept the use of beverage alcohol, such total sanctions are inappropriate and, moreover, fail to reduce significantly undesirable drinking behavior, not having been primarily designed with this in mind. The belief that there is something intrinsically wrong about all drinking and that all drinking is of one and the same type continues to influence attempts to control the use of alcohol.

The dilemma in dealing with alcohol problems is illustrated by the difficulties with alcohol education which confront public schools. While education about alcohol is often required by law,[1] a lack of agreement in most communities regarding the objectives and content of such education has allowed few schools to comply with the law in more than a token fashion. Should alcohol education point out the dangers of alcoholism, should it encourage abstinence, or should it emphasize moderation in drinking? Should it focus on drinking by juveniles or by adults? The inability of most communities to give teachers firm guidelines on such issues makes it almost impossible to carry on effective classroom alcohol education.

Strange temporary combinations sometimes develop in local elections centering on whether a community shall be "wet" or "dry." Abstinent church groups opposing the sale of alcohol on religious-moral grounds find themselves working with bootleggers who oppose the legal sale of alcohol because it would put them out of business. An analogous situation recently developed in New York State when efforts were made to combat the graft connected with inflated values of liquor licenses by ending the twenty-year freeze on the number of liquor outlets. This was opposed by some church groups and also by the organization of liquor store owners. The church opposition was based on a desire to promote moderation and to limit the amount of drinking which they believed would increase if the number of liquor stores increased, while the liquor store owners' association, in contrast, feared additional competition might endanger their economic position. In at least one area of the state, meetings were

1. These laws, almost without exception, were placed on the books during the late 19th and early 20th centuries in response to the demands of temperance workers. Many specify that there should be instruction on the dangers of alcohol. In recent years efforts have been made to bring alcohol education into conformity with current public attitudes toward drinking.

organized jointly by these two groups to oppose the legislation.[2] These examples illustrate the variety of interest
groups, the conflicting points of view that relate to questions of the use and abuse of beverage alcohol, and the
sometimes quite incompatible assumptions about causes
of problems in this field.

Perhaps the most important problem is the failure to see
the interrelatedness of diverse alcohol problems. Many
alcohol problems reflect disagreement on basic issues regarding beverage alcohol: is drinking "bad" in itself or
possibly dangerous; should it be postponed to later ages,
or minimized, or eliminated? What constitutes acceptable
or allowable drinking, and how can the other types of
drinking be discouraged?

Clashes between various interest groups have made virtually impossible the development of rational public policies on the use, sale, or distribution of alcoholic beverages.
Although the Temperance Movement in America now is
relatively weak numerically and financially, it still exerts
considerable influence on public policies concerning marketing and advertising, and on alcohol education. The
alcoholic beverage industry and government agencies concerned with liquor control often react as though confronted with the threat of a new and powerful Prohibition
Movement. The conflicts between "wet" and "dry" ideolo-
gies have been so energy-consuming that a detached examination of American drinking patterns and systems of
control and intervention has not been possible. Conclu-
sions about alcohol and drinking frequently seem to stem
directly from the mid-nineteenth-century philosophy of
the American Temperance Movement, which held that all

2. Reported in the *Jamestown* (New York) *Post Journal*, February 15,
1964.

drinking led to drunkenness and that reducing the availability of alcohol was the key to the control of all problems. People's beliefs and attitudes about alcohol and drinking are closely related to their general values and ethical views. That is, one's views on alcohol use are usually associated with other views, such as those regarding pleasure, gratification of needs, social relationships, and religious beliefs. This interrelatedness complicates efforts to modify attitudes and to stimulate action on these issues. It is one factor underlying the avoidance of broad discussions of alcohol problems and the preference for "keeping the lid on" this topic.

The lack of agreement about what amount of drinking is acceptable has contributed to the widespread neglect of problem drinking. There has also been confusion regarding the nature of alcoholism. It has been viewed as a "moral weakness," a disease, a symptom of underlying psychological disorder, and as a legal or social problem. The diversity of such views both reflects and reinforces the confusion, and leaves uncertain what should be done about problem drinkers and unanswered such questions as whose responsibility it is to provide assistance to these patients, what such assistance should consist of, what the effects of such assistance would be on others, and above all, how to deal with the larger issue of prevention.

The continuing discrimination against most problem drinkers, the low level of interest in their care and treatment, and the limited public and professional concern about this problem area, all reflect the general American ambivalence and confusion regarding alcohol use and abuse. Although a wide range of persons are involved in alcohol problems—the problem drinker and his family, his employer, "helping" or "care-giving" agencies, such as mental hospitals, general hospitals, clinics, welfare and social agencies, physicians, police, and clergy—there has been surprisingly little interest and activity directed toward providing assistance for these patients. Preventive approaches, especially those relating to altered drinking patterns in the American society, have received even less attention.

While many individuals are not uneasy about their own use of alcohol, there is much disagreement regarding matters of public policy. Americans prefer to avoid issues of this nature—they rarely are confronted with them. The result has been that undue prominence is often given to the views of two relatively small segments of the population—those concerned directly with the production, marketing, and sale of alcoholic beverages, and those opposed to all use of alcohol. The bulk of Americans, of course, do not fall into either of these two groups.

Most American efforts to deal with alcohol problems fail to view them in a broad context; instead, narrow, piecemeal, ineffective remedies for isolated parts are usually proposed. For example, confusing and often contradictory laws and regulations govern the sale of alcoholic beverages in different states and provinces. A number of states completely prohibit public sale by-the-drink;[3] in some states no alcoholic beverages, not even beer or wine, can be sold in supermarkets or grocery stores; in other states, these are found on the shelves of many retail food stores. Twenty-one years is the minimum age for purchase of alcoholic beverages in most states; in some, beer and wine may be bought at eighteen. Until recently in North Carolina, women were allowed to purchase alcoholic beverages at seventeen if they were married! Some states require bars to

3. Texas and North Carolina, for example.

provide food and other drinks; but bars in North Dakota are prohibited from serving coffee, milk, sandwiches, or hamburgers.[4] In many states, liquor stores and bars must close on Sundays; in others they stay open from six in the morning until after midnight seven days a week. In Pennsylvania, during the early 1960's, the legislature retained a law forbidding restaurant drinking on Sundays, but under pressure from the convention business, allowed alcohol to be served on Sundays in hotels.

These and myriad other rules and regulations strikingly confirm the lack of agreement on what types of legal controls are most likely to prevent the development of undesirable and harmful drinking practices. It is clear, however, that most of these statutes are based on the unproven theory that controlling the availability of alcohol is the major, if not the only, means of controlling drinking problems.

Some additional examples will illustrate the range and variety of alcohol problems. Several years ago in New York State there was much discussion about legislation to increase the number of retail liquor outlets and to remove minimum price restrictions on liquor. In 1966 several state legislatures, including those in California, Massachusetts, and New Jersey, had great difficulty deciding whether to adopt proposals requiring drivers to submit to tests for intoxication when stopped on the highway by the police.[5] In New York and in the states bordering on it there has

4. In North Dakota bars may sell only foods of "inconsiderable size or amount" (letter, January 26, 1965, from the State Attorney General to the North Dakota Beverage Dealers Association).

5. Under consideration were so-called "implied consent" laws, under which the driver's license would be suspended (or revoked) if he refused to take the test. Such laws currently exist in a number of states and the Supreme Court has declared them constitutional.

been much controversy about raising the minimum age in New York for the purchase of alcohol to twenty-one, while in some states there are suggestions about lowering the age to eighteen.

Still another alcohol problem receiving increased attention is the question of public drunkenness. Two recent court decisions,[6] barring criminal punishment of "chronic alcoholics" for public intoxication, have focused public attention on this issue. These decisions challenge the legal basis for the most frequently imposed sentence of the entire criminal code. If upheld by higher courts, they undoubtedly will have a substantial impact on a major American alcohol problem.

A very different kind of problem is the intense guilt that may be felt by a young person from a strongly non-drinking background who drinks, even if only moderately, under pressure from his peer group.[7]

The unique place of alcoholic beverages in American culture is evidenced by the fact that only one Amendment to the United States Constitution has ever been repealed; that was the Eighteenth, or Prohibition, Amendment. It remained in effect for slightly under fourteen years—from early 1920 to late 1933. The Prohibition Amendment was an attempt to "legislate morals"; repeal of the Amendment was taken as evidence that the American people felt this attempt had not succeeded, or indeed, was an example of the medicine's being even worse than the illness. The hos-

6. *Easter* v. *District of Columbia*, 361 F.2d 50 (D.C. Cir. 1966) and *Driver* v. *Hinnant*, 356 F.2d 761 (4th Cir. 1966). See p. 110, footnote.
7. See R. Straus, "Public Attitudes Regarding Problem Drinking and Problem Eating" in *Alcohol and Food in Health and Disease. Annals of the New York Academy of Science*, 133:792-802.

tile and apprehensive reaction to this particular means of regulation has unfortunately been transferred to the general idea of a comprehensive approach. As a result, proposals to change drinking patterns—whether by educational, legislative, or other means—are still likely to evoke charges of disregarding the "lessons" of the Prohibition experiment.

A further heritage of Prohibition has been a fear of reopening emotionally charged arguments associated with that experience. Most voluntary and governmental alcoholism programs have carefully avoided becoming involved in issues touching on general drinking patterns because of concern about being labeled "wet" or "dry." They have felt that such involvement would only detract from their primary tasks of gaining public acceptance of alcoholism as an illness, and of developing treatment services for patients. For this reason, alcoholism program workers have often publicly acted as though cultural attitudes about drinking and abstaining were not relevant to the provision of treatment services or to the prevention of problem drinking.

In very recent years, there has been public discussion again of preferred and harmful ways of using alcohol. Popular magazines no longer shy away from articles on alcohol; there is increased emphasis on the topic of social drinking and entertaining as well as on alcohol problems.[8] The passage of time since repeal of the Prohibition Amendment, the weakening of the Temperance Movement, and a more general acceptance of social drinking contribute

8. See the summary of the study by P. Kollings, "America's Search for a New Drinking Norm," in P. Verden, *Alcohol in America* (in preparation for the Cooperative Commission on the Study of Alcoholism).

to a climate favorable to the eventual development of a reasonable American alcohol policy.[9] It is now possible to consider ways of encouraging appropriate drinking behavior—and of discouraging other kinds—while still leaving people who wish to abstain entirely free to do so. This more reasonable approach means seeing that all drinking is not one and the same thing. Various Protestant denominations are moving closer together in their approaches to alcohol problems and have modified their traditional abstinence views.[10] There are also welcome signs that the alcoholic beverage industry is now ready to accept some responsibility for modifying drinking patterns. Recognition of various types of drinking leads to the further recognition that problems are associated with some types of drinking and not with others. This, in turn, allows for more discrimination, more effective planning and policy-making—in education, legislation, and personal decision-making.

9. A number of Protestant denominations that formerly opposed all drinking have now altered their stand and focus primarily on the necessity for moderation. Furthermore, some state temperance groups are emphasizing dangerous forms of drinking rather than concentrating on total abstinence.

A recent Gallup Poll indicated that "dry" sentiment is at its lowest point since Repeal. From 1936 to 1956 about one third, and sometimes slightly more, of the population favored legal prohibition. In the last ten years the figure has dropped to slightly over one fifth (22 per cent). Reported in the *San Francisco Chronicle*, February 28, 1966.

10. See T. Price, "The Churches and Community Education," *Special Report #27*, North American Association of Alcoholism Programs, Washington, D.C., undated (1966); and Q. L. Hand and J. T. Sanders, "Abstinence, Freedom and Responsibility," *Christian Advocate*, 10:11-12, 1966.

3

The extent of problem drinking

Large numbers of people in America use beverage alcohol in ways harmful to themselves or others. These patterns of problem drinking include the occasionally heavy-drinking young executive who becomes a hazard on the highway as he drives home after parties; the homeless Skid Row man who is repeatedly arrested for public drunkenness; and the white-collar or factory worker whose episodes of excessive drinking cause his family much suffering and who is on the verge of being fired either for absenteeism or for chronic problems while on the job.

The impact of problem drinking on several major "caregiving" agencies is reflected in the following statistics.[1] In 1964 there were slightly under 70,000 first admissions of male patients to the nearly 300 state mental hospitals in the United States. Over 15,000 patients, approximately 22

1. In most instances these figures probably grossly underestimate the number of problem drinkers in contact with a particular type of agency. There continues to be a strong tendency not to give the diagnosis of alcoholism to patients and clients. See, for example, I. Wolf *et al.*, "Social Factors in the Diagnosis of Alcoholism in Social and Non-Social Situations: II. Attitudes of Physicians," *Quarterly Journal of Studies on Alcohol*, 26:72-9, 1965.

per cent, were given a diagnosis of alcoholism at the time of admission.[2]

The story for psychiatric wards of general hospitals—which now admit almost twice as many patients annually as do the state mental hospitals—is much the same. In 1964, for example, 22 per cent of the men discharged from these community-based psychiatric facilities were diagnosed as "alcoholic."[3] Large numbers of problem drinkers receive at least minimal care in the medical and surgical wards of general hospitals. As many as one fourth of the patients in such wards may be problem drinkers, even though this condition is not usually the immediate cause of their admission.[4]

Problem drinking is found in a sizeable proportion—estimates range from 10 per cent to 25 per cent—of the families of welfare recipients.[5] This does not, of course, mean that drinking necessarily caused the indigency or its per-

2. *Patients in Mental Institutions, 1964: State and County Mental Hospitals*, U.S. Department of Health, Education, and Welfare, National Clearinghouse for Mental Health Information, Public Health Service Publication No. 1452, Part II, p. 21.

3. *Patients in Mental Institutions, 1964: Private Mental Hospitals and General Hospitals with Psychiatric Facilities*, U.S. Department of Health, Education, and Welfare. National Clearinghouse for Mental Health Information, Public Health Service Publication No. 1452, Part III, p. 41.

4. In one report 29 per cent of the patients were found to be problem drinkers, W. S. Pearson, "The Hidden Alcoholic in the General Hospital: A Study of 'Hidden' Alcoholism in White Male Patients Admitted for Unrelated Complaints," *North Carolina Medical Journal*, 23:6-10, 1962.

5. *Monthly Report Bulletin*, County of Westchester (New York), Department of Public Welfare, Vol. 4, No. 10, 1964; *Public Assistance Cases Where Alcohol Is a Factor Contributing to Need*, 1965: Wyoming State Department of Public Welfare; *Massachusetts Mental Health Planning Project Report*, Task Force on Alcoholism, Department of Mental Health, 1965; and D. K. Wass, "Public Welfare and the Drinking Problem," *Progress*, 6:64-8, 1964.

sistence. Professional workers in various helping fields frequently find many problem drinkers among their cases. Public-health nurses, social workers in family agencies, welfare workers, physicians in the emergency wards of general hospitals, parole and probation officers, clergymen, and lawyers report that problem drinking is one of the medical-social problems most frequently encountered in their day-to-day work. All—or nearly all—of these problem drinkers need help of some sort, and most behave in ways that cause concern to others in the community. Moreover, those in the immediate family, especially children, are most likely to be adversely affected.

Each year many people are arrested for public drunkenness in America. In 1965, of the total reported arrests for all offenses in the United States, slightly less than one third, 1,535,000, were for public drunkenness. However, several hundred thousand additional arrests listed in police records as disorderly conduct, disturbing the peace, vagrancy, and other charges, are commonly known to refer largely, and sometimes almost entirely, to public drunkenness. There were, in addition, over 250,000 arrests for drunken driving.[6] Police departments and criminal courts spend a significant proportion of their time dealing with alcohol-related problems. For example, the sixth largest category of arrests is "violation of liquor laws," and those offenses do not include drunkenness.

Police, safety, and health officials have long sought to call public attention to the problem of drinking and driving. A clear association has been established between the influence of alcohol and fatal motor-vehicle accidents. A

6. All figures from *Crime in the United States—Uniform Crime Reports—1965*. Federal Bureau of Investigation, U.S. Department of Justice, Washington, D.C., 1966.

recent well-designed study[7] established that among drivers responsible for fatal accidents drinking before driving was three times as frequent as among a comparable group of drivers not involved in such accidents. Equally striking is the finding that almost half—46 per cent—of the drivers in fatal accidents had very high blood-alcohol concentrations,[8] while none of the non-accident group had been drinking this heavily.

Figures such as these are only rough estimates. Many of them are known to be inaccurate because of poor records, or the failure to maintain any records on the subject. The arrest figures cited, for example, are without question gross under-reports; hospital admissions, death certificates, and welfare records are perhaps equally inaccurate. Non-reporting, under-reporting, or misleading reporting are clearly related to widespread community attitudes and provide a formidable barrier to rational comprehension and planning. Thus, despite the widespread occurrence of problem drinking, and the substantial contact that most persons in helping positions have with problem drinkers, only very limited provision of adequate assistance has been made available to these men and women. The problem drinker often creates bafflement, confusion, and anger, not only in those with whom he is closely associated but also in those who have some opportunity and responsibility to help him.

7. J. R. McCarroll and W. Haddon, Jr., "A Controlled Study of Fatal Automobile Accidents in New York City," *Journal of Chronic Diseases*, 15:811-26, 1962.
8. The levels were over 0.25 per cent—equivalent to 10 ounces of whiskey (six to nine drinks). See McCarroll and Haddon. However, it is clear that far lower levels of blood alcohol also present greatly increased risks of motor vehicle accidents. See also R. F. Borkenstein, *et al.*, *The Role of the Drinking Driver in Traffic Accidents* (Bloomington: Indiana University Press, 1964).

4

Past neglect of problem drinkers

In virtually all American communities, problem drinkers are likely to receive less adequate care than individuals with other kinds of difficulties. Furthermore, the patient suffering from alcohol intoxication is generally not treated with as much sympathy and competence as are most other patients. Often the actual medical care is minimal and sometimes only the immediate life-threatening symptoms are dealt with. In the United States substantial barriers persist in the admission of alcoholic patients to general hospitals. Prepaid hospitalization-insurance plans do not often include coverage for alcoholic conditions.

In most mental hospitals, the level of interest in problem drinkers is still very low. As a general rule, few psychiatrists and psychiatric clinics offer treatment for these patients. Public-welfare agencies, with a few exceptions, have not provided the type of financial assistance for indigent problem drinkers that is usually offered to other indigent people. Among almost all helping agencies there has been a tendency to "pass the buck" in relation to problem drinkers.[1]

A particularly inhumane instance of the general reaction to problem drinking is the handling of homeless, unattached men who are found in the Skid Row sections of all larger American cities. They are victims of the "revolving door" system that has prevailed for so many years: arrested for drunkenness, they are sent to jail for a short period and later released to the city streets, where they soon are arrested again on the same charge.

The unfounded belief that problem drinkers cannot be helped has accompanied and supported the limited interest in providing assistance for them. The belief persists despite ample evidence that many problem drinkers have been helped to control their drinking and to function again in the community. Large numbers have been helped through the efforts of Alcoholics Anonymous, and others by psychiatrists and other physicians, or by various health and welfare agencies. Numerous follow-up studies of the treatment of problem drinkers show recovery rates, based on both abstinence and improved social functioning, ranging from one third to two thirds of the patients treated. These figures compare quite favorably with results reported in the treatment of general psychiatric conditions and other behavioral problems.

In view of the magnitude of problem drinking, there has been only limited interest in research in the area. Substantial studies have not been undertaken by the many scientists in the disciplines most directly involved—medicine, psychiatry, and the social sciences. This lag in both

1. D. Pittman and M. W. Sterne, *Alcoholism: Community Agency Attitudes and Their Impact on Treatment Services,* National Clearinghouse for Mental Health Information, U.S. Department of Health, Education, and Welfare, Public Health Service Publication No. 1273, undated.

treatment and research has been paralleled by the virtual disregard of problem drinking in the curricula of professional training institutions. Medical schools, along with schools of nursing and social work, have virtually ignored it.

Few individuals or groups have been interested in or willing to fight for the rights of problem drinkers to humane care and appropriate treatment. These patients have no broadly based national lobby. Both the National Council on Alcoholism and the North American Association of Alcoholism Programs have attempted to function in this role, but have not as yet had the desired impact on the public or on governmental agencies or the major professions.[2] Even Alcoholics Anonymous, whose contribution in calling attention to the magnitude and neglect of alcoholism has been of singular importance, focuses primarily on helping individuals rather than attempting to deal with alcoholism as a community or public-health problem. Problem drinkers do not generally evoke sympathy; indeed their frequent drunkenness evokes just the opposite reaction in most situations. Then too, these individuals often do not themselves ask for help, not only because they may be unaware of the true nature of their condition, but because they are aware of the typically punitive and essentially unhelpful responses to their condition.

General health and welfare agencies, governmental as well as voluntary, must become sources of leadership if substantial progress is to be made in providing better care and treatment for the problem drinker. Such agencies will probably have to assume *primary* responsibility, although valuable contributions can be made by specialized alcoholism programs.

2. See p. 179.

One major goal of this report is to help develop a better climate for discussion and research and action on *all* aspects of alcohol problems. A second goal is to improve the care and rehabilitation of problem drinkers. The third objective is prevention, that is, to reduce the rates of problem drinking.

There is an urgent need for improving treatment services. For too long problem drinkers have been neglected by most helping agencies. Such people should have the same rights and access to care and treatment as others in need of help. However, even if the discrimination were overcome, it is unlikely that sufficient services could ever be developed to provide adequate *care* for all, and only widespread efforts to *prevent* problem drinking hold out the promise of a long-range solution.

Up to the present time, no broadly conceived programs for dealing with problem drinking have been developed in America. Treatment activities are usually piecemeal or otherwise inadequate, even in areas with substantial alcoholism programs; moreover, very little is generally done about prevention. An effective national program will require the coordinated participation of many different agencies, organizations, and workers, and the appropriation of substantial additional funds.

A national policy concerning alcohol use, directed primarily at reducing problem drinking, is presented. It will be seen that while additional knowledge is urgently needed, much can be done on the basis of existing information.

5

Recent developments

Only during the last thirty years have any concerted efforts been made to deal with problem drinking. This slow development was climaxed in March 1966, when President Lyndon B. Johnson referred in some detail to alcoholism in his Health and Education Message.

The founding of Alcoholics Anonymous in the mid-1930's helped to spur public and professional interest. Alcoholics Anonymous is a voluntary, loosely knit organization of problem drinkers who regularly meet in small groups to help one another to remain sober and to function effectively in society. Emphasis is placed on mutual aid and self-help; there are no professional employees nor are there any formal relationships with governmental or other agencies.

At the scientific and professional level a major stimulus was provided by the work of the Research Council on Problems of Alcohol, which was organized in the mid-1930's. This was followed in 1939 by an important literature revie w[1] and in 1940 by the founding of the *Quarterly*

1. E. M. Jellinek, ed., *Alcohol Addiction and Chronic Alcoholism* (Yale University Press, 1942).

Journal of Studies on Alcohol at Yale University. During the 1940's the Yale Center of Alcohol Studies, the Yale Summer School of Alcohol Studies,[2] and the first "Yale Plan" alcoholism clinic were established at New Haven. Also during these years, tax-supported alcoholism programs were established in a number of states and provinces—sometimes through the effective political lobbying of individual members of A.A. In 1944 the National Council on Alcoholism (originally the National Committee for Education on Alcoholism) was organized through the efforts of the Yale group and Mrs. Marty Mann, its current executive director. The Council is the national voluntary health organization in the field of alcoholism. There are local alcoholism committees or councils in close to one hundred communities, most of which are affiliated with the National Council.[3]

In the 1950's a number of additional states and provinces set up alcoholism programs, and at the present time forty states and seven Canadian provinces have specifically designated programs. While most of these programs originally were organized as independent boards or commissions, in recent years many have been integrated into other state agencies—particularly departments of mental health and public health. Currently about one fourth of these state programs exist as independent commissions or boards.[4] The budgets of the state programs generally have been

2. Now both at Rutgers, the State University, New Brunswick, New Jersey.

3. See p. 181 for a further discussion of the National Council on Alcoholism.

4. In four Canadian provinces alcoholism programs exist as government-supported "foundations." These include the largest specialized program in North America, the Ontario Alcoholism and Drug Addiction Research Foundation.

rather small, especially during their first years of existence, and they have usually attempted to provide only token treatment services for problem drinkers. The efforts of state alcoholism programs to stimulate interest and action on the part of other governmental agencies and voluntary health and welfare agencies have had only limited success.

The North American Association of Alcoholism Programs was established in 1949 as a voluntary organization composed primarily of the administrators of state and provincial alcoholism programs. The Association, which now also accepts for membership any person interested in alcohol problems, currently functions as a communications center for state and provincial programs and their personnel.

In 1956 the American Medical Association issued a statement urging physicians to provide care and treatment for alcoholics, reiterating that alcoholism was an illness.[5] For many years the A.M.A. has had a Committee on Alcoholism (now the Committee on Alcoholism and Drug Abuse) under its Council on Mental Health, and a number of state medical associations have also established committees on alcoholism. The American Public Health Association has in recent years greatly expanded its activities relating to problem drinking. While these activities undoubtedly have had an impact on physicians' attitudes and practices in relation to treating problem drinkers, much more work is needed in this area.

In the last few years there have been a number of significant developments relating to alcoholism. Extensive federally initiated mental health planning (1963 to 1965) included attention to alcoholism in many states. Many

5. See Appendix A for the text of this statement.

newly established community mental health centers[6] have as one of their responsibilities the treatment of problem drinkers. In 1965 the American Psychiatric Association issued a strongly worded statement on the role of psychiatrists in providing help for problem drinkers.[7] These trends in the field of mental health are mirrored elsewhere.

Public-health departments—at state and national levels—have begun to urge their workers to pay more attention to alcoholism and other types of problem drinking. State and local public-welfare agencies are also striving to develop more humane policies and effective services for public-assistance recipients who are problem drinkers. At the federal level, an intradepartmental committee on alcoholism, established by the Secretary of the Department of Health, Education, and Welfare, has made recommendations regarding the role of various units of the Department. A National Center for Prevention and Control of Alcoholism has been established within the National Institute of Mental Health. Hearings on alcoholism were held in the fall of 1965 by a committee of the House of Representatives, and legislative pressure for federal action has been increasing. An International Congress on Alcoholism will be held in the United States for the first time in the fall of 1968.

A small, but increasing number of industries have begun to develop alcoholism programs for their employees. Such programs often include: (1) a specific company policy on

6. Limited federal funds for construction and personnel for these centers are authorized under the Community Mental Health Center Act of 1963 and the Mental Retardation Facilities and Community Mental Health Centers Construction Amendments of 1965. Legislation currently before Congress proposes continuing federal support for state and local mental health programs.

7. See Appendix C for the text of this statement.

how problem drinkers are to be handled; (2) a system of referring problem drinkers to industrial health departments; and (3) an educational program about alcoholism for the supervisory staff. While management-operated alcoholism (or mental health) clinics are generally opposed by industrial health and trade-union officials, a few industrial establishments have set up special treatment programs for the problem drinker. These are often strongly influenced by A.A. philosophy. These developments all suggest that there now is increased readiness to improve the care and treatment provided for problem drinkers.

Since the end of World War II major religious groups have become concerned about alcoholism and other drinking problems. These include the Roman Catholic Church as well as some large Protestant denominations. For example, among Presbyterians, Episcopalians, and Methodists, there has been not only an increasing concern about alcoholism, but also a change in attitude toward social drinking, with the tendency to distinguish between acceptable and unacceptable drinking. Church groups have also become interested in alcohol education, particularly for young people. While some efforts retain their distinctive emphasis on abstinence, others now stress the potential dangers of *certain* kinds of drinking.

II

Treatment and management of problem drinking

1

Introduction

A basic belief of our civilization is that suffering should
be relieved, regardless of the person, his contribution to
society, or the manner in which the suffering was brought
about. Many problem drinkers require care to relieve their
suffering and yet are often unable to obtain such assistance. An additional belief of our culture is that treatment
to prevent further suffering and to restore physical and
social functioning should be provided.

The many different opinions, views, and theories about
the nature of alcoholism determine, in a major way, how
persons with this particular illness are treated, how they
are handled by helping agencies, and how they are regarded by the public. Policy about problem drinking is
greatly influenced by public belief. Misinformation, preju-
dice, and ignorance about the nature of problem drinking
itself, or regarding the treatment of individuals with this
difficulty, have often hindered or set back efforts to care
for these patients.

The provision of treatment to problem drinkers is complicated because they differ from one to another in so

many ways. Not only do their drinking patterns vary greatly, but also their physical health, psychological condition, and economic circumstances. Some need immediate attention to their physical health problems, others require primarily individual psychotherapy for emotional difficulties, while for some, vocational readjustment is an urgent need. It is rare to find a problem drinker who does not also have other difficulties besides his problem with alcohol. Some of these will be related to the drinking (either as causes or as consequences), while others merely co-exist in the same individuals without any particular relation to the difficulties with alcohol.

Therefore, in planning treatment services for problem drinkers, or in developing a treatment plan for an individual, it is necessary to take into account more than just the drinking; in fact, it may even be impossible to deal with the drinking behavior unless other problems are also tackled. And even when patients are helped to control their drinking, the other problems often remain and may be neglected if the sole focus has been on the drinking. It is necessary also to take into account the patient's social matrix: most problem drinkers are involved with, affect, and are affected by other persons. A sound treatment policy requires that an overall assessment should be made of each patient's physical, social, and economic deficits and assets, as well as of his drinking problem.

The goals of treatment for most conditions are the relief of symptoms and the restoration of health. However, in alcoholism the situation is complicated by the fact that few, if any, problem drinkers will be able to return to "normal" social drinking. Thus the term "cure" is usually avoided. Abstinence, or at least altering the patient's drinking patterns, is generally the primary objective. Often this must come before progress can be made in other areas; however, long-term control over drinking frequently cannot be achieved without other significant changes in the patient and his situation, including a reduction of tensions and distress. The abolition or reduction of drinking is often an inadequate goal. The quality of the patient's life, his interpersonal relations, and his social and psychological functioning, must all come within the focus of treatment.

For some chronic problem drinkers realistically limited goals must be set. Improved social functioning, even without the cessation of drinking or much change in the drinking behavior, may represent a significant achievement. The number of "episodes" of uncontrolled drinking may be reduced with a consequent reduction of physical and social damage to the patient and others. Improved family relations, fewer arrests for drunkenness, a reduction in days of hospitalization, or less time lost from work, are examples of limited gains whose importance should not be minimized.

For many years it was believed that problem drinkers could not be helped by professional treatment. In spite of increasing evidence contradicting this view, strong pessimism still persists in some circles. The general conflict in American culture over alcohol use has helped maintain this attitude of "therapeutic nihilism," and the ambivalence of physicians and many other helping agents toward these patients has interfered with their providing adequate assistance and treatment. Strong residual feelings that alcoholism is a self-inflicted condition and that the inability to control one's drinking is a sign of moral weakness or inadequacy often reinforce beliefs that these persons are neither worthy of nor responsive to help. These attitudes also influence reactions to "successful" and "unsuccessful" cases. The latter are vividly recalled and the former may be forgotten. The "slips" of problem drinkers are more likely to be considered evidence of failure than are comparable setbacks of other patients. Large numbers of problem drinkers have, of course, been helped by professional agencies, by physicians, and by Alcoholics Anonymous.[1] In addition, there are people who have had serious drinking problems for a number of years and then stopped having difficulty with alcohol without assistance from either A.A. or a professional source of help. Such spontaneous recoveries are, of course, not unknown in psychiatry and other fields. The continued persistence of pessimistic views about the treatment of problem drinkers reflects the strength of public and professional ambivalence about alcohol use and abuse.

1. See pp. 62-4, "The Unique Role of Alcoholics Anonymous."

2

Causes of problem drinking

Theories about the causes of problem drinking are various and complex. They include difficulty in managing personal anxieties or tensions, although this characteristic is naturally not limited to problem drinkers. Social processes can play a significant role in stimulating excessive drinking, in fostering its non-recognition, or in keeping it under control. Altered metabolic processes may also influence drinking behavior. While much additional information is still needed on the nature and causes of problem drinking, existing knowledge has yet to be fully applied. Heart disease, cancer, schizophrenia, and delinquency are not completely understood either, yet a community which responded to these conditions as it responds to problem drinking would be considered medieval and a national disgrace.

DEFINITION OF PROBLEM DRINKING

For the purposes of this report, problem drinking is a *repetitive use of beverage alcohol causing physical, psy-*

chological, or social harm to the drinker or to others.[1] This definition stresses interference with functioning rather than any specific drinking behavior. The actual amount or frequency of drinking is not a primary criterion. The definition will, moreover, vary in its application because standards of appropriate and inappropriate behavior or of adequate social functioning vary from group to group, and among different social classes and cultures. For example, a man who is not required to keep regular working hours may continue to function effectively in his occupation even while drinking very heavily; for another, with regular working hours, the same kind of drinking behavior would have serious consequences. If a man's drinking does not interfere with social functioning, and if it has no harmful effects on his own physical and mental health or on that of others, he would not be considered a problem drinker.

There are some repeated uses of alcohol causing "harm to others" that are qualitatively so different that they require special mention. For example, an abstinent, "anti-alcohol" wife may be sufficiently upset by her husband's daily drinking of two glasses of beer that her psychological health is "harmed." By the above definition this man would have to be considered a problem drinker. Yet while his drinking in the face of his wife's strenuous objections may indicate that much is wrong in the marital relationship, his "problem with alcohol" is very different from that of other persons who repeatedly are drunk or otherwise incapacitated because of drinking. Similarly, a man in an extremely

---

1. This is a broad definition which includes the condition called "alcoholism." The various views and definitions are examined in greater detail by M. Levin in Chapter V of *Alcohol Problems and Public Policy* (in preparation for the Cooperative Commission on the Study of Alcoholism).

poverty-stricken family may be "harming" his wife and children through the money he spends on alcohol, even though he never becomes drunk, or otherwise alters his behavior by drinking. A crane operator who regularly drinks a bottle of beer at lunch may be endangering the safety of his fellow workmen because of the slight impairment to his coordination and judgment resulting from drinking.

Most of these situations require some sort of intervention—more often of a legal, disciplinary, or controlling than of a "treatment" nature. However, such examples are exceptions, and the bulk of persons classified as "problem drinkers" by this definition clearly need care and treatment.

DEFINITION OF "ALCOHOLISM"

For the purposes of this report, alcoholism is defined as a *condition in which an individual has lost control over his alcohol intake in the sense that he is consistently unable to refrain from drinking or to stop drinking before getting intoxicated.* This is by no means an entirely adequate definition; however, the element of lack of control appears to characterize a sufficient proportion of problem drinkers that it can be used as a criterion for alcoholism, though the proportion of problem drinkers who fall under this definition is not known.

The term "loss of control" usually includes two different phenomena. The first is the inability to do without alcohol or to manage personal tensions without drinking, often called the "inability to abstain." The second is the inability to stop drinking after one starts. Some physiological bases have been suggested for this difficulty, such as seeking to avoid the withdrawal symptoms.[2] However, no adequate physiological explanation has yet been given of some persons' apparent need to return to drinking (the inability to abstain), even after not having had a drink for days or weeks. This type of drinking behavior is often described as "psychological dependency."

The inability to abstain is not an all-or-none phenomenon, that is, individuals with this problem do not drink every day or whenever they can get a drink. The psychological state of the person and the particular social situation influence whether the person will drink or not. Many people, for example, described as "alcoholics" experience little or no difficulty managing without alcohol while they are in a protected setting, such as a nursing home, a hospital, or a penal institution. Thus, persons with this condition do not always become intoxicated once they begin drinking; a variety of circumstances influences whether or not the first drink leads to the second, and so on. Loss of control cannot then be conceived as an automatic process that operates independent of psychological and social factors.

The term "alcoholism" has been used in different ways. Some definitions have been very broad and all-inclusive. The World Health Organization in 1955, for example, concluded that alcoholism is a "collective term" for a "family

2. Withdrawal symptoms may occur when there is a reduction in the concentration of alcohol in the blood and central nervous system. The most frequently reported symptoms of withdrawal are restlessness, tremors, sweating, and nausea. Inability to sleep, depression, anxiety, convulsions, and hallucinations may also occur. These symptoms are usually most dramatically apparent when the drinking ceases, but they can also develop with merely a reduction in the rate at which alcohol enters the circulatory and nervous systems.

of problems correlated to alcohol."[3] The late E. M. Jellinek, one of the foremost scholars of alcohol problems, suggested that for operational purposes, alcoholism be defined as "any use of alcoholic beverages that causes any damage to the individual or society or both."[4]

The use of the term "alcoholism" to describe so many varied conditions probably is not desirable, however. It may lead to stereotyping and to a gross oversimplification of highly complex phenomena. The diversity of the people included under the term of "alcoholism" may be concealed and consequently disregarded. Using the term in a more restricted sense, as is done here, is not fully satisfactory either. There is the danger that distinctions will then be sharply drawn between persons with alcoholism and other problem drinkers, and that only the former will be thought to merit or require sympathetic care and treatment, or that only after their needs are met should attention be given to other problem drinkers. The position of this report is that both groups require and merit help, and that neither group should be given preference.

The term "alcoholism" should be used with the awareness that this condition is not always easy to diagnose or to be distinguished from other types of problem drinking. In addition, even those to whom the diagnosis is correctly given still differ greatly from one another and are likely to require different types of treatment and assistance.

3. World Health Organization, *Alcohol and Alcoholism: Report of an Expert Committee*, W.H.O. Technical Report Series, No. 94, Geneva, 1955.
4. E. M. Jellinek, *The Disease Concept of Alcoholism* (New Haven: College and University Press, 1960), p. 35.

VIEWING ALCOHOLISM AS A HEALTH PROBLEM

While alcoholism may be seen as a social, a behavioral, or an ethical problem, for present purposes it is useful to view it as a health problem. The health view has been important in helping to counteract the long-standing belief that persons with alcoholism are morally inadequate people who have willfully brought problems on themselves through their own weakness or sinfulness. Seeing alcoholism in a medical health context has made it possible to substitute helping or healing in place of the punitive and judgmental approaches of the past. Many research studies that have been conducted within medical health and social-science settings would probably not have been undertaken had former concepts of the nature of alcoholism still been as prevalent.

This report approaches alcoholism as a "health problem" and places it in the perspective of a comprehensive view of health, that is, a view stressing the multiplicity of factors which may initiate and determine the course of the alcoholism. In addition to physiological factors, it considers psychological and social factors and the sociocultural environment. This comprehensive view suggests that there is no single cause of alcoholism, even though all affected persons may have some common symptoms. Furthermore, there probably is no single preventive approach or treatment for all cases.

In recent years, some questions have been raised about viewing alcoholism as a disease. It has been argued, for example, that to most persons—laymen as well as professionals—the term "disease" connotes specific biochemical or physiological disturbances. Critics of the "disease" concept fear that the use of this term may lead many to view alcoholism as a homogeneous disease entity caused by specific biochemical or physiological disturbances; they therefore recommend that alcoholism *not* be regarded as a "disease" in that limited medical sense. This argument illustrates that the newer "comprehensive health view" has not yet been totally understood or accepted by the public and even by some professional workers.[5]

The term "alcoholic" is avoided here because it can readily lead to oversimplification and stereotyping of problem drinkers. Labeling someone as "alcoholic" implies that the person's major characteristic is thus being described, as if other elements of his physical, psychological, and social functioning were relatively unimportant. The oversimplification which assumes that all drinking and all drinkers are "one and the same thing" has somehow been transferred to the label "alcoholics." There are many types of "alcoholics," and this lack of discrimination between types is as damaging to treatment policies as is the lack of discrimination between different types of drinking and drinkers to the development of effective programs for alcohol problems in general.

The term "addiction" has frequently been applied to

5. An analogous point is made in the final report of the Joint Commission on Mental Illness and Mental Health, ". . . one way around the impasse of public and professional attitudes that we appear to have erected would be to emphasize that persons with major mental illness are in certain ways different from the ordinary sick. Information embodying this new emphasis would require an explanation of why they are different and also an explanation of why society behaves as it does toward the mentally ill. With such an understanding, it might be possible to proceed in the light of fuller reason to adopt more helpful attitudes." *Action for Mental Health* (New York: Basic Books, Inc., 1961), p. 85. For further comments about the comprehensive health view, see Chapter V in *Alcohol Problems and Public Policy*.

alcoholism; however, it is often used without specifying whether the reference is to a strictly pharmacological concept or to a more loosely defined psychological one. In regard to addiction, the World Health Organization's Committee on Alcohol and Alcoholism in 1955 designated ethyl alcohol as a drug "intermediate in kind and degree" between "habit-forming drugs" and "addiction-producing drugs."[6] In his summary of this argument Jellinek[7] stated that the reason for assigning alcohol to this intermediate position was largely the quantitative differences between alcohol and the addiction-producing drugs. He pointed out that the latter produce addiction in 70 to 100 per cent of their users. He further noted that the amounts required to bring about this effect are minute, and the time required for the addictive process is 2 to 4 weeks. Jellinek contrasted this with alcohol consumption which leads to addition in a maximum of one per cent of the users, requires large amounts (several thousand times larger than morphine, heroin, or barbiturates), and in which the time necessary for the addictive process is 3 to 20 years.

More recently, another World Health Organization Committee has suggested that there are numerous types of "drug dependence." This term is used in preference to "addiction." It is felt that "drug dependence" is a far broader term covering a variety of conditions including the "barbiturate-alcohol type." This condition is said to exist when

> the individual's consumption of alcohol exceeds the limits acceptable to his culture, when alcohol is consumed at times that are not deemed appropriate in that culture, or when the intake of alcohol becomes so great

6. World Health Organization, *op. cit.*
7. Jellinek, *op. cit.*, p. 118.

as to cause damage to the health of the drinker or impairment of his social relations. Since use of alcoholic beverages is a normal, or almost normal, part of the culture of many countries, dependence on alcohol is usually apparent as an exaggeration of culturally accepted drinking patterns, and the manifestation of dependence varies accordingly in a characteristic fashion with the cultural mode of alcohol use.[8]

Definitions of this type seek to do justice to the social, psychological, and physiological components of the condition.

Alcoholism then is considered an "illness" in the light of a comprehensive health view which includes an awareness of: (1) the multiplicity of causal factors; (2) the probable existence of many different courses of development (rather than a single course of development); and (3) the need to utilize a variety of treatment and preventive approaches, non-medical as well as medical.

CAUSES OF PROBLEM DRINKING

Psychological and social factors are of major importance in the development and persistence of alcoholism and other types of problem drinking. Clinicians experienced in helping problem drinkers frequently report that these patients have an unusual amount of stress and much deprivation in their lives. It has been noted that these patients have often been unable to develop close and meaningful interpersonal relations. They also experience difficulty in tolerating frustration and in controlling their impulses. Such characteristics are, of course, not unique to problem

8. N. B. Eddy, H. Halbach, H. Isbell, and M. H. Seevers, "Drug Dependence: Its Significance and Characteristics," *Bulletin, World Health Organization,* 32:721-33, 1965.

drinkers, but are found among many persons, especially those with psychological difficulties. The reliance on drinking as a means of dealing with personal tensions and discomfort points to the possible key role of psychological factors in the development of the drinking problem. Furthermore, the apparent relationship between emotional crises and changes in drinking patterns suggests that psychological elements play an important role in problem drinking. Thus, while the psychological characteristics that differentiate problem drinkers from persons with other kinds of behavioral problems have not yet been ascertained,[9] many experts do agree that psychological factors are important to the development and persistence of problem drinking, and even that individuals with certain personality traits are more likely to become dependent on alcohol than others.[10]

Some problem drinkers report that their physiological and psychological reactions to alcohol were unusual from the first.[11] This is in contrast to many others who drank "normally" for a period of years before their drinking patterns changed.[12] These variations in initial reactions to

9. Even if substantial common psychological elements were found it could not be shown that these existed prior to the development of the drinking problem. They might have arisen as a consequence of years of heavy drinking, and of experiences associated with this, such as the responses of others in society to the problem drinker.

10. One of the reasons for the failure to discover specific psychological or physiological characteristics in research studies may be the grouping together under the heading "alcoholism" of persons with very different kinds of drinking problems. The heterogeneity of this sample would make difficult, if not impossible, the task of finding any common elements among these persons.

11. E. M. Jellinek, "Phases of Alcohol Addiction," *Quarterly Journal of Studies on Alcohol*, 13:673-84, 1952.

12. M. Bailey, and B. Leach, *Alcoholics Anonymous, Pathway to Recovery: A Study of 1,058 Members of the AA Fellowship in New York City*, National Council on Alcoholism, 1956.

alcohol may be based on biochemical physiological factors. However, there is no evidence that this is so, and thus, evidence regarding the possible causal role of these factors in the initiation of alcoholism or other types of problem drinking is inconclusive.

While many who have been heavy drinkers for years may exhibit health problems, such as liver cirrhosis, endocrine or gastric dysfunction, or neurological complications, there is no clear evidence that these conditions existed prior to the initiation of the problem drinking. Some long-term problem drinkers develop withdrawal symptoms on the cessation of a drinking episode. While theories have been developed regarding the physiological bases of these withdrawal reactions, they are not yet fully understood. Certain problem drinkers have been reported to metabolize alcohol differently than do normal social drinkers. Other than occasional findings of this nature, no consistent physiological differences have been noted as yet between problem drinkers and non-problem social drinkers.[13]

While problem drinkers are found in all strata of American society—among all occupational groups, in rural as well as urban areas, and in virtually all religious denominations—there are variations in rates of problem drinkers in different areas of the country, and among different religious and ethnic groups. There are, of course, problem drinkers also among women in the United States and Canada, but the rates are generally about five times as high among men as among women. Alcoholism tends to occur most frequently among those aged 35 to 55. The slow development of the drinking problem over a period of many years is a major reason for this age distribution.

13. See a recent review article, D. Lester, "Self-Selection of Alcohol by Animals, Human Variation, and the Etiology of Alcoholism." *Quarterly Journal of Studies on Alcohol*, 27:395-438, 1966.

Substantial differences in rates of problem drinking have been noted in different cultural groups—both in the United States and Canada, and in other parts of the Western world. While there are obviously variations in the ways in which these rates have been estimated, the differences reported are so striking and consistent that they cannot be disregarded. In the United States higher rates of problem drinking are found among persons from Irish and Anglo-Saxon backgrounds than among those of Italian, Chinese, or Jewish backgrounds. It is of interest to note that in the first two groups the ways of teaching youngsters the "rights" and "wrongs" of drinking are far less clearly defined than in the other groups.[14] In traditional Italian-American, Chinese-American, and Jewish families, much clearer distinctions are usually made between drinking that is not acceptable and drinking that is; there is rather consistent disapproval of drunkenness.[15] In addition, these groups generally introduce young people to alcoholic beverages in the home in a relatively routine and unemotional manner. The relationship between differences in attitude toward normal drinking and different rates of problem drinking strongly suggests that the nature of *drinking patterns* (and associated attitudes) can influence the extent of *problem drinking* in a cultural group. However, only a

14. See D. D. Glad, "Attitudes and Experiences of American Jewish and American Irish Male Youth as Related to Differences in Adult Patterns of Insobriety," *Quarterly Journal of Studies on Alcohol*, 8:406-27, 1947.
15. See, for example, J. Skolnick, "A Study of the Relation of Ethnic Background to Arrests for Inebriety," *Quarterly Journal of Studies on Alcohol*, 15:622-30, 1954; M. Barnett, "Alcoholism in the Cantonese of New York City," in *Etiology of Chronic Alcoholism*, O. Diethelm, ed. (Springfield, Ill., 1955); and C. R. Snyder, *Alcohol and the Jews: A Cultural Study of Drinking and Sobriety* (New Haven: Publications Division, Yale Center of Alcohol Studies, and Glencoe, Ill.: Free Press, 1958).

small minority of drinkers, even among those of Anglo-Saxon or Irish-American background develop drinking problems, and it is clear that other factors besides membership in a particular cultural group are involved. There are also, of course, problem drinkers among Jews, Chinese, and Italian-Americans.[16]

Clearly, people would not become problem drinkers in an alcohol-free society. In this sense the alcohol is a necessary condition for the development of problem drinking. On the other hand, since the vast majority of alcohol users do not become problem drinkers, other factors—biological, psychological, and sociological—must be involved in the development of the disorder.

A tentative model may be developed for understanding the causes of problem drinking, even though the precise roles of the various factors have not yet been determined. An individual who (1) responds to beverage alcohol in a certain way, perhaps physiologically determined, by experiencing intense relief and relaxation, and who (2) has certain personality characteristics, such as difficulty in dealing with and overcoming depression, frustration, and anxiety, and who (3) is a member of a culture in which there is both pressure to drink and culturally induced guilt and confusion regarding what kinds of drinking behavior are appropriate, is more likely to develop trouble than will most other persons. An intermingling of certain factors may be necessary for the development of problem drinking, and the relative importance of the different causal factors no doubt varies from one individual to another.

16. See R. Wilkinson, *The Prevention of Alcoholism: "Liquor Control" and Public Education* (a report in preparation for the Cooperative Commission on the Study of Alcoholism), for a further discussion of these issues.

There are great differences in individual responses to alcohol, as to virtually all other substances or stimuli. Some persons become sleepy, others tense and excited, when they drink. Some find it a pleasant experience, others a distressing one. These differences may be at least partly physiological. Then, too, individuals differ in their psychological make-up, in the quality and intensity of their conflicts, and in their ways of dealing with emotional tensions and anxiety. And finally, as has been indicated, there are variations in the meanings attached to drinking and to drunkenness, whereby in some cultures, drinking symbolizes group solidarity; in others, it is an institutionalized way of releasing inhibitions; and in still others, it takes on special meanings, such as proof of manliness.

NEED FOR RESEARCH

Additional information about the nature and causes of problem drinking is urgently needed. Past research in this area has been uneven and sporadic. Many investigators have undertaken one or two studies relating to alcohol use and then have ceased working in this field.

A wide range of studies is relevant to problem drinking: included are research on pathological alcohol use, investigations of normal (or social) drinking in different cultural groups, and studies of the impact of legal and other controls on drinking behavior. Research is needed on the physiological action of alcohol, on brain functioning, on neurophysiology, and on neuropharmacology. There are also opportunities for significant research having to do with the problem uses of alcohol; for example, the long-term effects of alcohol on the central nervous system, the liver, and other organs require further investigation. The precise nature of the withdrawal process is not understood either; nor are the phenomena referred to as "dependence" and "loss of control."

Although drinking clearly has various meanings for different individuals, relatively little is known about the psychological and social functions of both normal and deviant drinking. The meaning of drinking probably also varies among subcultures and between different groups in the same culture. How do different social groups maintain control over drinking behavior and under what circumstances does this control break down? What is the relation between customary drinking patterns and the nature of problem drinking in various subcultures? Answers to such questions are needed to obtain a better understanding of the overall place of alcohol use in different social institutions, and to assist in the development of improved treatment, educational, and preventive programs.

Longitudinal (long-term) studies can contribute greatly to a better understanding of the role of physiological, psychological, and sociocultural factors in the development of various kinds of problem drinking. Retrospective (historical) studies probably cannot provide this kind of information. Methods of early case-finding may, for example, be developed on the basis of longitudinal studies; such studies, therefore, while generally very costly, are probably an essential element of a broad national research effort. Large-scale longitudinal studies should perhaps focus on several disorders and conditions and not be restricted to a single one, such as schizophrenia or alcoholism; financial support might then be more readily obtainable for work on more than a single diagnosis.

Many of the types of studies needed in relation to alcohol, alcohol use, and drinking problems are inseparable from basic, and even applied, research in other areas. Undoubtedly, as further general progress is made in both the biological and social sciences, much will be learned that applies directly to problem drinking and to alcohol problems in general. Investigations focusing on alcohol-related questions can also contribute knowledge that is relevant to other areas, such as basic physiology, personality functioning, and group and sociological phenomena. While special attention to alcohol problems is currently required because of the long-standing neglect, research in this field cannot be developed in isolation from investigations of a basic-science nature and those on other medical and psycho-social problems.

3

Current alcoholism treatment services

Public attitudes and feelings about drinking and about alcohol abuse have significantly influenced the way services for problem drinkers have developed. The belief that the problem drinker cannot be helped—sometimes referred to as "therapeutic nihilism"—and the view that the condition is "self-inflicted" result in the problem drinker's frequently being ignored by most helping agencies and by many professional workers.

Hospitals, psychiatric agencies, public-welfare departments, and social agencies, among others, are often reluctant to provide care and treatment for problem drinkers; they tend to neglect or reject them. An understanding of the nature of problem drinking and its management are often limited in such helping agencies. Certain services generally available to patients with other disorders are frequently denied to problem drinkers by policy or practice. These include hospital insurance coverage, admission to general hospitals, assistance by public-welfare agencies, voluntary admission to mental hospitals, and participation in most mental hospital after-care programs.

Where care and treatment are provided to problem drinkers they are often narrow and segmented; that is, adequate assessment of the patient's total problems and potentialities is lacking and only limited aspects of the patient's life situation and various problems are dealt with. Continuity of care is absent, especially between inpatient and outpatient services and between medical services and behavior-oriented ones. Agencies serving problem drinkers generally prefer to work with the most motivated, best educated, and the most socially intact patients. Usually little care and treatment are provided persons most lacking in these characteristics. Finally, the specialized alcoholism services—special programs in mental hospitals, alcoholism clinics, and half-way houses—are often isolated from the other community helping agencies.

As has been indicated earlier[1] very large numbers of problem drinkers are in contact with one or more major American helping agencies, including general hospitals, mental hospitals, and public-welfare agencies; however, there is much variation in the actual treatment these patients receive from the different agencies. Some agencies, such as public-welfare departments, rarely provide any help to these patients for their drinking problems.

This chapter will give a brief overview of general American helping agencies, which is followed by a description of the four major types of care for problem drinkers—(1) emergency services, (2) inpatient care, (3) outpatient care, and (4) transitional facilities—and by a discussion of the unique role of Alcoholics Anonymous. The chapter also includes a discussion of the issue of motivation.

1. See pp. 17-20.

GENERAL AMERICAN HELPING SERVICES

American helping services have developed in a rather haphazard fashion, and there are still severe problems of coordination and considerable inadequacies in community planning. Medical care is provided primarily by physicians in private practice and (in the United States) by voluntary hospitals. While in the past much of the medical care for indigent and near-indigent persons has been provided by free clinics and municipal and county hospitals, this may change rapidly in the United States with new federally supported medical care programs. State and local public-welfare agencies provide financial assistance to indigents under several categories of federally supported programs. General assistance (without federal subsidy) is provided by states and localities[2] to those not eligible for the specific programs. Voluntary family agencies,[3] which in the past also supplied considerable financial assistance to the needy, currently focus mainly on counseling, homemaker services, and other types of specialized assistance.

Inpatient psychiatric care is still provided principally by state mental hospitals, although an increasing number of patients are now admitted to and receive short-term care in the psychiatric wards of general hospitals, municipal and county as well as voluntary. Outpatient psychiatric clinics have expanded greatly in the last twenty years and

2. There is, however, great variation among states and even within states in the eligibility requirements and benefits for the general assistance programs. Similar variation in eligibility and benefits also occurs in the federally supported programs.
3. These agencies are supported primarily by contributions from individuals and through the local United Fund.

currently number 2000 in the United States. These are usually tax-supported and are staffed by teams of psychiatrists, social workers, and psychologists. Community mental health centers are a recent development. These facilities—and there are only a few at present—provide a broad range of mental health services—inpatient care, outpatient care, 24-hour emergency care, after-care for hospitalized patients, partial hospitalization (during either daytime or nighttime hours), and consultative services for other community agencies.

Different problems arise as a result of this haphazard organization of services. Many agencies often operate in isolation from one another and frequently view patients only in terms of the particular services they are providing. Patients may be receiving care from several agencies with little or no communication between agencies to coordinate the services. Also serious is the loss of continuity of care when a patient is discharged by one agency and requires further assistance from another. Often too, agencies have not established mutually agreed-upon policies regarding the transfer of cases, intake procedures, and which types of clients are to be served by different agencies. Finally, in most American communities there is inadequate planning of health and welfare services; that is, new services are established without adequate assessment of community needs to determine the most urgent priorities for additional services. These general—and very serious—inadequacies of American helping services should be kept in mind in discussing the care provided persons with drinking problems.[4]

4. A more detailed discussion of treatment services for problem drinkers and of related issues will be presented in S. Cahn and T. Plaut, *The Nation's Therapeutic Services in Disarray: A Case Study of Services for Problem Drinkers* (in preparation for the Cooperative Commission on the Study of Alcoholism).

EMERGENCY SERVICES

There are six principal settings in which care is provided for the acute consequences of excessive alcohol intake: (1) emergency rooms (and wards) of general hospitals; (2) psychiatric wards of general hospitals; (3) special detoxification facilities; (4) mental hospitals; (5) patients' homes or offices of private physicians; and (6) jails and police "lock-ups." The needs of intoxicated patients range from life-saving measures to deal with hepatic compensation, gastro-intestinal bleeding, fluid imbalance, and deep coma, to a sheltered place to "sleep off" the effects of the alcohol. The prevention of delirium tremens and other alcoholic psychoses (or their treatment if they do develop) is a major objective in the medical care of acutely intoxicated persons. The provision of this emergency medical care is technically not very difficult, and it is shocking that deaths due to acute intoxication still occur.

1. *Emergency Care in General Hospitals.* Large numbers of intoxicated persons appear at or are brought to the emergency services of voluntary and municipal general hospitals. Here they may wait for a long period of time before receiving care: accident victims and other patients often receive priority. There is great variability in the care provided intoxicated patients; those on the verge of delirium tremens or close to a coma—that is, in life-threatening circumstances—generally obtain emergency care. Others, particularly if they fit the stereotype of Skid Row men, are likely to receive only minimal medical attention.

Most hospitals are reluctant to admit intoxicated persons, particularly if they are indigent, to the general medical wards unless absolutely necessary. Patients with the same symptoms resulting from another toxic condition usually have no difficulty obtaining inpatient care. Patients with insurance coverage, or other financial resources, can usually obtain hospital care through the efforts of a private physician. Sometimes the physician will use a covering diagnosis, labelling the patient's condition, for example, "gastritis" or "severe indigestion" to get around hospital policy or to protect the reputation of the patient and his family.

The treatment typically provided in general hospitals is very limited; in most cases it deals only with the patient's toxic state and other urgent medical problems. Rarely are attempts made to deal with the drinking problem or to develop a plan for the patient's continuing treatment. Referral to psychiatry, or social service departments, or to other community agencies, including A.A., is also rare. The "crisis" of hospitalization and acute illness is not, then, used as an opportunity for beginning treatment of the patient's fundamental problem, his drinking. The reappearance of the same patients in the emergency wards with the same symptom—intoxication—reinforces the negative attitudes of the physicians, nurses, and attendants toward problem drinkers.

2. *Emergency Care in Psychiatric Services of General Hospitals*. Patients with alcohol intoxication account for over 20 per cent of male admissions in many emergency psychiatric services.[5] In some hospitals, admissions are directly to the psychiatric service; in most, however, patients first come to the emergency medical services. The average duration of stay is short, less than a week. Patients diagnosed

5. See footnote 2, p. 18.

as having brain damage may remain longer before being transferred to a state mental hospital, and a few others may also be sent to the mental hospital, but these constitute only a small fraction of all problem drinkers admitted to psychiatric wards. The treatment is primarily physical; sedation and drugs are used to manage the detoxification and to handle agitated behavior. Psychiatric treatment is rare, as is referral to psychiatric clinics or to other community agencies.

3. *Emergency Care in Special Detoxification Units*. Generally found only in major metropolitan areas, they specialize in providing medical and nursing care for severely intoxicated persons. Some are licensed hospitals, but most are not. There is usually not 24-hour physician coverage nor is around-the-clock nursing coverage always found. Hospitalization insurance is applicable in only a few of these institutions.

Many detoxification facilities are run by individual members of Alcoholics Anonymous and maintain close ties with community A.A. groups. There is generally little, if any, contact with other community agencies. The bed-occupancy rate of these facilities is usually quite low; rarely are more than half the beds in use.

4. *Emergency Care in Mental Hospitals*. If there is no local provision for emergency psychiatric care, the nearest mental hospital is likely to receive many intoxicated problem drinkers. In some mental hospitals, patients with "alcohol intoxication" as their diagnosis account for over 20 per cent of all male first admissions. There is much variation between states and within states in the policies of mental hospitals regarding the admission of these patients. Some

hospital superintendents feel that detoxification is primarily a non-psychiatric responsibility which should be undertaken by general hospitals rather than by psychiatric institutions; others view the mental hospital as the patient's last resource and are far more open in their admissions policy. Many mental hospitals, however, try to discourage the admission of intoxicated persons by informing the police and other agencies that they will not accept them.

Duration of stay in mental hospitals for patients admitted with an "alcohol" diagnosis is usually relatively short—one to two weeks as a rule—except in hospitals where there are special alcoholism units. Patients are usually admitted on a voluntary basis, that is, not committed, and since little effort is made to persuade them to stay for protracted psychiatric treatment, some leave the hospital as soon as the medical crisis is passed. Under such circumstances it is virtually impossible to make plans for further treatment or for referral to community agencies.

5. *Emergency Care by Private Physicians.* Undoubtedly a large, but unknown, number of intoxicated persons are cared for by private physicians, either in the patient's home or in the physician's office. Alcohol intoxication can often be handled on an outpatient basis if treatment is begun early enough and if someone is available to provide nursing care between visits to the doctor.[6] Some physicians are reluctant to make house calls—even if they already know the patient and his family; such patients also may not be welcome in the doctor's office because of concern about the reactions of other patients in the waiting room.

6. A. L. Ruprecht, "Day-Care Facilities in the Treatment of Alcoholics," *Quarterly Journal of Studies on Alcohol*, 22:461-70, 1961.

Because of these attitudes some local alcoholism commit-tees[7] have set up lists of physicians who are willing to at-tend such patients.

6. *Emergency Care in Jails.* More men are "dried out" in jails—where good medical care is rarely available—than in all other kinds of facilities combined. Each year most large cities have several deaths of intoxicated prisoners. Many who are arrested for public drunkenness spend a night in jail or police "lock-ups" and are then immediately released or appear before a judge. Some judges will send very ill prisoners to correctional institutions, where they may re-ceive minimal medical care while serving a short sentence. Most jails have arrangements for the immediate transfer of very sick prisoners to a local hospital. The jail cells for intoxicated prisoners are usually very crowded, quite crude, and totally inadequate from both a humane and medical standpoint. The infamous "drunk tanks" found in almost all city jails are instances of barbaric mistreatment. The fault is not primarily with the law-enforcement agen-cies; police departments and jail personnel generally do not feel that these men are criminals. The responsibility rests with the community, which, having failed to develop an alternate way of handling the problem, generally man-ages the problem by "sweeping it under the rug" in the local jail, thereby hiding it from the general population and from community leaders.[8] Recent court decisions bar-ring the jailing of "chronic alcoholics" for the offense of public drunkenness will perhaps force a re-evaluation of this problem. Eventually, it may be treated on a medical rather than a criminal basis.

7. See p. 179 ff for a discussion of citizens' groups.
8. See p. 110 ff for a further discussion of public drunkenness.

The actual medical management of alcohol intoxication, while requiring experience and skill, is not a task of overwhelming difficulty. Some psychiatric receiving hospitals have treated thousands of cases without ever having had a death attributable to the alcohol itself. Many deaths due to intoxication in jails and hospitals are needless; that they nevertheless occur is a severe indictment of the medical profession and community leaders alike for permitting these conditions to persist. The full potentialities of non-institutional (outpatient) care for management of the acute effects of alcohol also have not been developed. Medical and technical knowledge is available, but not the necessary organizational and institutional arrangements.

All detoxification services should undertake diagnostic assessments of patients, and referral to appropriate community therapeutic resources for the drinking problem should be an integral part of such services.

As community mental health centers become focal points for the provision of psychiatric care—including emergency care—the management of detoxification may change, especially as a consequence of the court decisions regarding the jailing of public drunkenness offenders. If, as has often been proposed, mental health centers are either located in, or closely affiliated with, community general hospitals, the development of adequate medical, psychiatric, and social services for these patients should become feasible.

THE UNIQUE ROLE OF ALCOHOLICS ANONYMOUS

The fellowship of Alcoholics Anonymous has had an immense impact on public attitudes and on professional programs for problem drinking. Alcoholics Anonymous stresses that alcoholism is a disease and that persons suffering from it have lost their ability to control their drinking. There is a strong spiritual quality to the A.A. philosophy, with a heavy emphasis on moral values and personal reform; self-help and mutual aid are key elements. The frequent meetings consist principally of the study of A.A. principles, and of members giving personal reports on their own successful struggles in dealing with alcoholism. In addition, members do "Twelfth Step" work, giving individual assistance to other problem drinkers and carrying the A.A. message to them. The apparent effectiveness of A.A. has helped to counteract the belief that problem drinkers cannot overcome their drinking difficulties. The clearly stated rules and principles of A.A. have been a help to many problem drinkers, although serving as a barrier for some others. The stress on acknowledging their helplessness has enabled many problem drinkers finally to stop denying that their drinking was a problem they could not control. On the other hand, some people are unable to make this type of admission of personal inadequacy.

Some elements of Alcoholics Anonymous—some of its day-to-day operations and the attitudes of many of its members—have come into conflict with professional agencies. Many in A.A. feel strongly that there is no need for other services and programs (except for medical management of the toxic effects of alcohol) in the rehabilitation of problem drinkers. On the other hand, some segments of the public and some community care-givers expect A.A. to assume the major role in the rehabilitation of these persons. The existence of A.A. is even used at times to justify the absence of professionally directed services.

In the field of problem drinking, as in many others, self-help organizations can significantly supplement professional forms of assistance. Up to now Alcoholics Anonymous has been different from most other mutual aid groups because of the "all-purpose" function it has sought to fulfill. There have been some significant changes, however. Many A.A. groups and individual members are now less antagonistic toward problem drinkers who seek help from professional agencies, and some actively encourage the seeking of such help.

Although A.A., in its role as a mutual aid group, has been of outstanding importance in the rehabilitation of problem drinkers, it has not reached more than a small proportion of problem drinkers in any community, nor can more be expected. Psychiatrists and other physicians, social workers, and other care-giving personnel, as well as legislators, judiciary, and police, should view A.A. in perspective, appreciating its extraordinary and unique contribution but recognizing the limits of applicability of its principles and practices and also the necessity for professional services. Alcoholics Anonymous is the outstanding twentieth-century example of a self-help group but it is not the cure-all for problem drinking.

INPATIENT CARE

Inpatient care refers to residential treatment which seeks to change the patient's drinking behavior, rather than that dealing primarily with the immediate medical effects of excessive drinking. The major service for this type of care in the United States is the *state mental hospital*.

Large numbers of problem drinkers are admitted annually to the 285 state mental hospitals in the United States. As many as 40 per cent of all men admitted to the mental hospitals in some states are given a diagnosis of alcoholism.[9] Approximately five times as many men as women are admitted to mental hospitals with this diagnosis. Nearly half of the patients are between the ages of 45 and 64 and almost half are admitted on a voluntary rather than on a committed basis.

Approximately 10 per cent of the state hospitals have special alcoholism wards or programs, some of which provide very good care and treatment for problem drinkers. Of the hospitals with alcoholism programs, most have a special unit for these patients; others have special daytime alcoholism programs, but the patients live together with other patients in the general psychiatric wards. The majority of mental hospitals, however, do not have any special program and often little or no treatment is provided for problem drinkers—at times not even the therapeutic services available to other patients. Problem drinkers are often kept for longer periods of time in some hospitals so that they can perform maintenance and other jobs.

Although most of the mental hospital alcoholism wards do have some form of medical supervision, the responsibility for administration of the units is not always in the hands of physicians. Many programs are directed by non-medical personnel—particularly social workers, psychologists, and nurses. In some hospitals, recovered problem drinkers—usually members of Alcoholics Anonymous—are the major treatment personnel and often have a significant impact on the therapeutic philosophy of the staff. The stimulus behind the development of the special programs has varied; usually the interest of one member of the hospital staff has provided the original incentive. State mental

9. *Statistics Newsletter,* State of Maryland, Department of Mental Hygiene, VII, No. 8, 1966.

health departments have only rarely taken a leadership role in initiating the alcoholism programs.

In addition to A.A. meetings the two most frequently used therapeutic approaches in the wards are: (1) group psychotherapy and (2) didactic lectures, discussions, and movies. Sometimes the two approaches blend. Group therapy (or discussion) is usually conducted on a daily basis by various members of the staff. The focus varies, but the emphasis is often on helping patients to verbalize their feelings about themselves, their situations, and their drinking, with the objective of giving them a better understanding of the psychological and social factors responsible for their drinking behavior.

In most alcoholism wards the staff actively encourages patients to continue discussions about their drinking problems on an informal basis outside of the group meetings. A similar emphasis on the patient's major problem area outside the formal therapeutic situation is not found in most general psychiatric treatment programs. The stress in Alcoholics Anonymous on keeping the drinking problem—and the need for abstinence—before the patient has been carried over to many programs in mental hospitals. Virtually all programs include regular A.A. meetings. Attendance is usually not obligatory, but considerable pressure may be exerted to have the patient attend at least once.

Lectures, slides, tapes, and movies on alcoholism are part of the regular therapeutic program in most hospitals. Sometimes films and lectures on general topics, such as emotional disorders and personality development, are also included. The widespread use of didactic approaches like these is quite striking. In part they are based on a belief that problem drinkers need to have an intellectual understanding of their condition; that with such understanding a patient can consciously exert substantial control over his drinking. The didactic methods also attempt to increase the patient's motivation for help, as well as the desire to alter his way of life.

"Therapeutic community" and "milieu therapy" concepts are applied in many alcoholism wards. These two terms refer to a treatment philosophy that emphasizes using the patient's total daily experience as part of efforts to improve his psychological functioning. Efforts are made to create an atmosphere in the hospital ward that will maximize the patient's potential for recovery. All hospital personnel, including attendants, are expected to be part of the "treatment team." Patients are allowed to wear their regular clothing and to mix freely with other patients. Patient government is frequently used both as a means of involving patients in the day-to-day operations of the unit, such as making decisions about minor disciplinary matters and sometimes major ones, arranging for assignments of work, making rules about the use of television, and so on, and as a means of helping patients enhance their self-esteem and learn new ways of dealing with authority. Often emphasis is placed on the democratic character of the unit, and patients are treated as individuals with rights and responsibilities of their own rather than as sick people who need to be cared for. The morale of both patients and staff in many alcoholism wards is high—there is a spirit of mutual cooperation and a belief that the patients receive significant help from the staff and from one another.

Most alcoholism wards do not accept patients directly; admission is made through the regular hospital admission procedures, and the unit staff then select those newly admitted patients thought to be appropriate for the special program. There is a strong tendency to prefer younger patients, or those with fewer hospital admissions, with more evidence of adequate social functioning (job and family status), or of higher education levels. Relatively few socially isolated Skid Row men are found in the special alcoholism wards. If such patients do obtain admission to the mental hospital they often do not get into the alcoholism units.

In most general mental hospital wards, intensive individual psychotherapy is not regularly used. In part this is so because of the shortage of personnel, but it may also reflect a professional opinion that individual psychotherapy is not appropriate for many of these patients. Staff members are usually available for private discussion, and such discussions do take place, but the whole procedure is radically different from the psychotherapy usually found in outpatient clinics or in private practice.

Many alcoholism wards use sedatives and tranquilizers during the first days or weeks of the patient's stay in the unit. Vitamin injections are often given to help the patient physically. Generally, however, the hospital staff seeks to have the patient entirely free of medication long before release from the hospital.

When the mental hospital is located close to a major urban area, and therefore near the homes of many of its patients, efforts may be made to involve the patient's family in the treatment process. However, the absence of contact with families, by the hospital staff or community agencies, is a major shortcoming of many mental hospital alcoholism programs. But the situation is no better for other patients in mental hospitals.

The most serious shortcoming of the alcoholism programs is the almost total absence of after-care and follow-up programs and activities. Rarely are arrangements made for patients to continue treatment with a community agency after their release from the hospital. The hospital staff does not have time for this work; it may not be familiar with these resources, and there are often few (if any) such resources available in the patient's home community. Although the after-care of general mental hospital patients remains poor, problem drinkers are sometimes not included in whatever limited after-care activities exist. On the other hand, collaboration with public-welfare agencies in relation to indigent or homeless patients is found increasingly in alcoholism units; some even try to place a patient in contact with an A.A. group in his home community before his release from the hospital.

In too many hospitals the alcoholism units make only minimal use of other departments in the hospital, such as psychology, social service, vocational rehabilitation, occupational therapy, recreational therapy, and religious counseling. In addition, psychiatric residents, psychology interns, social work students, and nursing trainees are not often assigned to these wards. This contributes to the isolation of the alcoholism program from the rest of the hospital and reflects the relatively low status that such a program has within the total hospital system. Other hospital personnel are usually happy to have the alcoholism unit available, but do not themselves want to become involved in the program.

SOME SPECIAL TREATMENT METHODS

A number of special treatment methods are being used on an experimental basis by certain therapists and facilities—especially in mental hospitals. They include aversive conditioning, hypnotherapy, group psychodrama, and most recently, lysergide (LSD) therapy. None of these methods has been adopted on a large scale, but further investigation of the effectiveness of each will probably continue. Aversion therapy relies on classical or modified conditioning procedures to produce a disagreeable association (conditioned response) with alcohol. In one procedure the patient drinks an alcoholic beverage in close timing with the intake of an emetic which causes nausea and vomiting. After a series of such conditioning experiences, if the patient attempts to drink he will have the nauseous reaction even without the emetic. In other procedures the conditioned association may be produced by electric shock or hypnotic suggestion. However, many patients are not suited to such procedures. Aversion treatment is used often in combination with psychotherapy. Some patients have remained abstinent for many years after conditioned aversion experiences.[10]

Hypnotherapy has been used by a few psychiatrists and physicians, either by itself or in conjunction with psychotherapy. Suggestions are made to the patient under hypnosis that he will no longer feel any need or urge to drink. Sometimes, however, hypnosis is used to permit release of memories and to serve as a means for increasing patient-therapist interaction. The applicability of hypnosis in treating alcoholism, as in general psychiatric practice, is limited because not all persons can be hypnotized and because there are individual differences in responses to the post-hypnotic suggestion.

Psychodrama is based on the theory that the acting out of present, past, or future painful situations will lessen fear

10. See, for example, F. Lemere and W. L. Voegtlin, "An Evaluation of the Aversion Treatment of Alcoholism," *Quarterly Journal of Studies on Alcohol*, 11:199-204, 1950.

and give greater insight into the problem, especially if the participating audience gives its opinions, support, and even advice. The psychodrama director gives patients the courage to act out various feelings toward one another. This method has been used primarily with middle- and upper-class problem drinkers. However, some mental hospital alcoholism units are also using psychodrama sessions as part of their treatment program.

The use of lysergic acid (LSD) is a new approach to the treatment of problem drinkers. LSD, a strong hallucinogenic drug, alters states of consciousness. Under its influence patients have different feelings about themselves and others and report that their approach to life is dramatically altered.[11] Some investigators state that the drug can lead to major changes in psychological functioning. There are reports of problem drinkers apparently becoming more receptive to other forms of psychologically based treatment following one or more experiences with LSD. The use of this drug requires definite precautions from both medical and psychiatric standpoints. At present, there is considerable controversy as to whether science has demonstrated that LSD is therapeutically promising as a treatment for problem drinkers; however, it is likely that further experimentation will continue, at least until there are more conclusive findings about its effectiveness.

In summary, the alcoholism programs in mental hospitals represent a significant and major effort to provide inpatient treatment for problem drinkers. However, such

11. Recent reports of the experimental use of LSD in the treatment of problem drinkers include: H. Abramson, "Lysergic Acid Diethylamide (LSD-25) III. As an Adjunct to Psychotherapy," *Journal of Psychology,* 39:127-55, 1955, and C. M. Smith, "Some Reflections on the Possible Therapeutic Effects of the Hallucinogens," *Quarterly Journal of Studies on Alcohol,* 20:292-301, 1959.

programs exist in only a minority of mental hospitals, and where they do exist, they generally serve only a minority of problem drinkers admitted to these hospitals. Despite the many shortcomings—under-staffing, inadequacy of after-care arrangements, isolation from the rest of the hospital, a possible overemphasis on didactic approaches to the exclusion of others, and some instances of rigid ideology regarding treatment—there is much that other mental hospitals and newly developed community mental health centers can learn from these programs. Community mental health centers have an opportunity to improve greatly the types of alcoholism programs now found in most hospitals; in addition, they can work more closely with other agencies, both during and after the patient's hospitalization. The availability of day and night hospital services and of outpatient clinics will also be a tremendous advantage.

Relatively few problem drinkers receive treatment in special *alcoholism hospitals* or in *private psychiatric hospitals*. Both kinds of facilities are found in most parts of the country, but the total number of beds and days of patient care given is very small compared to state mental hospitals. Special hospitals and private psychiatric facilities provide longer care for detoxification and some treatment also for the drinking problem. These hospitals usually require payment in advance, and thus most patients, particularly in the psychiatric hospitals, tend to come from upper economic strata. Some of the special hospitals, however, provide quite inexpensive care. The "treatment" generally consists of tranquilizers and other drugs. A.A. meetings are held in some of these hospitals. While the admitting physician may continue a previously established relationship with the patient during the period of hospitalization, there are generally no organized treatment programs. Often in this type of program the emphasis is on physical detoxification rather than on handling the problem drinking with its varied socio-psychological components.

There are a small number of *non-medical rehabilitation facilities* for problem drinkers. These offer quite inexpensive care, usually for specified periods of time, such as three or four weeks. In the past the therapeutic orientation of these facilities has been primarily along the lines of Alcoholics Anonymous, but recently some have begun to introduce professional personnel and to develop programs similar to those in the special mental hospital units. Except for their close ties to A.A. groups, these facilities are usually isolated from other community agencies; however, they often have some arrangement with local hospitals to provide medical care for acutely ill patients and arrange medical coverage through local physicians.

Large numbers of problem drinkers, arrested for public drunkenness, end up in *prisons, jail farms,* and other *correctional institutions*. Most of these facilities provide, at best, a minimum amount of medical care; a few have regular A.A. meetings; fewer still are endeavoring to develop formal rehabilitation programs. Such programs are generally in a rudimentary stage, however, and provision for after-care following release is practically non-existent, except through A.A. The full impact of recent court decisions regarding the jailing of "chronic alcoholics" has not yet been felt by most courts. If these decisions become applicable throughout the United States there are likely to be major changes in the medical care provided to those arrested for public drunkenness.

OUTPATIENT (CLINIC) CARE

The two major sources of outpatient help for problem drinkers are alcoholism clinics and general psychiatric clinics. In addition, a great many patients (how many is unknown) receive help from physicians in private practice and from Alcoholics Anonymous.

The number of *alcoholism clinics* has greatly increased in recent years; at present there are more than 130 such clinics in the United States, most of which, however, do not operate on a full-time basis, and many of which are open only several half-days each week. The vast majority of these clinics are psychologically oriented in their general treatment methods, drawing their principal staff members from the mental health professions—psychiatry, psychiatric social work, and clinical psychology. Some of the alcoholism clinics are directed by social workers and psychologists; however, part-time psychiatric consultation is always available. Also, most of the actual treatment is provided by psychiatric social workers, who constitute the largest number of full-time and part-time staff members.

Although most alcoholism clinics use group therapy, for both patients and relatives, the primary therapeutic methods continue to be individual psychotherapy, casework, and counseling. This therapy is in many ways similar to that of psychiatric clinics, although the personnel of alcoholism clinics are often more active and directive in their work with the patients. In the psychotherapy, stress is placed on helping patients understand the psychological bases of their problems. There is often considerable time spent analyzing the patient's current family and work situations in terms of the anxiety, tension, and anger that they arouse, and the therapist assists the patient in examining his own feelings so that he may exercise more control over them. While therapists are aware of the importance of early childhood experiences, and will explore the meaning of these with the patient if they are brought up, the emphasis is more on the current difficulties.

Group therapy is conducted in various ways. The focus is generally on the patients' drinking behavior and the underlying social and psychological factors; but in some clinics relatively little attention is paid to the drinking, and discussion centers more on general psychological difficulties and problems in adjustment. Working with family members is considered very important by most alcoholism clinics. In this respect they are more like family agencies or child-guidance clinics than general psychiatric clinics. Some alcoholism clinics will work with the non-alcoholic spouse even if the problem drinker is not coming for treatment; however, efforts are made to involve this person as soon as possible. —

A striking feature of most alcoholism clinics is their willingness to make at least some provisional contact with the patient right away. Although there are often "waiting lists" for admission to treatment, a clinic staff member is almost always available to see the patient at least briefly within a day or two after initial contact with the clinic. The importance of making this first interview early is stressed, and a crisis-intervention philosophy is found in alcoholism clinics more often than is the case in the general psychiatric clinics. Only a very small proportion of patients (10 to 20 per cent) making contact with the alcoholism clinics show up for as many as five visits, but this is equally true of general psychiatric clinics and of child-guidance agencies. There is a tendency for the less educated, more socially disabled, and less motivated patient to drop out before a significant relationship is established.

Alcoholism clinics are similar to general mental health clinics in that they tend, in a variety of ways, to screen out those patients who seem unable to avail themselves of the particular types of therapy offered by the clinic. Patients labeled as poorly motivated and not "sincere" in their desire to do something about their drinking problems often are not accepted for treatment.[12] Greater imagination and experimentation are needed in alcoholism clinics to develop therapeutic approaches that are suited to the patients who do not now receive treatment.

While some clinics will close the case of a patient who misses a number of interviews, often the policy is to keep cases "open"; this is partly based on the notion that alcoholism is a recurrent chronic disorder in which the crises must be handled on the spot, and that patients need to feel free to return for help whenever they wish. Some patients do require "propping up," especially at times of crisis.

Although the alcoholism clinics usually stress to patients that they will have to give up alcohol, many therapists have other goals beside abstinence for their patients: there is concern for the overall psychological and social functioning of the patients. When patients have "slips" (begin drinking again), the staff does not see it as evidence of failure. In this sense, the treatment goals are broader than in many state hospital programs. The problem drinking is viewed in the context of the total personality, and attention is directed at helping patients improve their functioning in familial and occupational roles.

Most clinics make some provision, even if only minimal,

12. See p. 80 ff for a discussion of the question of motivation.

for medical care. A number of alcoholism clinics have nurses on their staff to supply patients with vitamins or other medication on the advice of a clinic physician. While the clinics generally are not at all equipped to handle acutely ill patients, they offer more medical services than do most general psychiatric clinics. Many clinics prescribe tranquilizing drugs for some patients. In some clinics certain patients may receive only limited psychotherapeutic assistance and come in periodically for medication and vitamin injections. Usually, however, the tranquilizers are used in conjunction with psychological assistance. Disulfiram, a drug that will, when taken regularly, cause the patient to become quite sick if he drinks alcohol, is used on a selective basis with a minority of patients.[13]

A major shortcoming of most alcoholism clinics is their relative separation from other community agencies. This is generally true of psychiatric clinics also. Contacts with family agencies, psychiatric clinics, local welfare agencies, vocational rehabilitation agencies, and the like are still mainly on a very limited basis. Some alcoholism clinics are used as field placements by schools of social work, but the majority are not. It is extremely rare to find psychiatric residents spending time in an alcoholism clinic. Few alcoholism clinics have any arrangements with nearby hospitals to take over and provide continuing treatment for pa-

---

13. Disulfiram (the generic name for Antabuse) must be taken regularly for it to function as a "pharmacological barrier" against the intake of alcohol. It does not reduce the patient's psychological need for alcohol; but the physiological reactions to alcohol, if the patient has regularly been taking disulfiram (or one of several other alcohol-reaction-provoking substances), are very unpleasant. This threat is sufficient to enable some patients to refrain from drinking. However, if patients feel they cannot manage without alcohol they have only to stop taking the tablets for three or four days.

tients after they are released from the hospitals, nor do alcoholism clinics generally have any procedure for receiving patients from community hospitals that provide detoxification care—either in medical or psychiatric emergency services.

Most clinics will refer some patients to Alcoholics Anonymous, although it is rare for an alcoholism clinic to associate itself directly with A.A. by, for example, providing space for group meetings on its premises. Also, in contrast to mental hospital alcoholism units, very few clinics have recovered problem drinkers as staff members.

The "success" rate of alcoholism clinics appears to be comparable to that of general psychiatric cases in mental health clinics. This finding applies whether the criterion used is the ability to "hold" patients in treatment (for at least five interviews) or whether it is the staff's assessment of improvement.[14] Both these criteria are, of course, of limited usefulness in assessing long-term therapeutic effectiveness. Evaluation studies of treatment, difficult as they may be, are essential for alcoholism clinics as well as for general mental health services.

Some of the strengths of alcoholism clinics are their availability to patients, their work with families, their flexibility in combining traditional psychotherapy with other approaches, and their increased use of group methods. Among the major weaknesses are the failure to provide real treatment for a substantial proportion of patients having at least an initial contact with the clinic; the lack of experimentation to develop new approaches for working with the less verbal, lower-class patient; the continuing

14. See A. K. Bahn, C. L. Anderson, and V. B. Normal, "Outpatient Psychiatric Clinic Services to Alcoholics, 1959," *Quarterly Journal of Studies on Alcohol*, 24:213-26, 1963.

isolation from other agencies—particularly general psychiatric services, mental hospitals, and medical detoxification facilities; and the lack of relationship with basic professional training institutions. A different kind of shortcoming of alcoholism clinics is the total avoidance of all other alcohol problems, and their failure to consider the field of prevention. Probably the most serious shortcoming of all is the very small number of such clinics.

Almost as many problem drinkers receive treatment in *general psychiatric clinics* each year as in the specialized clinics.[15] Even though only a tiny fraction of the patients in general clinics are problem drinkers, there are more than ten times as many general psychiatric clinics as alcoholism clinics. Generally, the psychiatric clinics report lower rates of success with these patients than do the specialized clinics. It cannot be determined from current information whether this reflects different therapeutic methods, different characteristics of the patients treated in the two types of clinics, different criteria of "success" (perhaps the psychiatric clinics are more likely to interpret a single "slip" as evidence of failure), or a real difference in effectiveness.

General psychiatric clinics usually prefer not to work with problem drinkers; some have explicit policies excluding them. Often the clinic staff does not feel qualified to work with such patients or they question whether psychological treatment can be effective. Psychiatric clinics are even less likely than alcoholism clinics to receive problem drinkers from the emergency medical services or from mental hospitals. As psychiatric clinics become an integral part of community mental health programs, they should

15. It is estimated that alcoholism clinics and general psychiatric clinics each provide treatment annually to about 20,000 problem drinkers.

begin to work with more of these patients and their families and to develop close collaborative relationships with existing alcoholism clinics.

THE ISSUE OF MOTIVATION

Among virtually all services that provide treatment for problem drinkers, much importance is attached to motivation.[16] In most agencies the key screening criterion is the patient's motivation (or sincerity) in wanting to stop drinking. Very few facilities are interested in working with patients they define as inadequately motivated. It is often assumed that motivation is an all-or-none phenomenon: well motivated, the patient is thought ready for treatment; otherwise, nothing is done until the patient decides he wants to stop drinking—as though the motivated patient were worthy of assistance and the non-motivated one not. (The same concern about a patient's "readiness" is found in Alcoholics Anonymous groups, where reference is made to persons not yet having "reached bottom.") The earlier attitude of rejecting all problem drinkers has been shifted to an acceptance of those who fit a certain image.

The tendency to blame the patient when treatment fails needs to be replaced by the view that each such occurrence is a challenge for the therapist and the agency to develop more effective techniques. It is too easy to dismiss an unfavorable outcome as evidence of the patient's lack of motivation; this is an abdication of professional responsibility. If current approaches and techniques are effective with only a certain proportion, further study and the de-

16. D. J. Pittman and M. Sterne, "Concept of Motivation: Sources of Institutional and Professional Blockage in the Treatment of Alcoholics," *Quarterly Journal of Studies on Alcohol*, 26:41-57, 1965.

velopment of new methods and approaches are required. Evidence is accumulating that changes in the organization, operation, and treatment philosophy of an agency can have a substantial effect on its ability to work with the supposedly unmotivated patient. For example, recent work at the Massachusetts General Hospital[17] has demonstrated that such changes increase both the number of referred patients who come to a clinic for treatment and who remain in treatment. Frequently too, the use of motivation as a criterion for the screening of patients functions so as to exclude those from variant cultural backgrounds, particularly persons from lower socio-economic strata who are not comfortable with the whole style of operation of most clinics, which is geared to middle-class clients. These clinics usually emphasize talking about one's problems, involving other family members in the treatment, and coming in at a fixed time every week—all of which may be quite alien concepts to many lower-class persons.

17. M. Chafetz et al., "Establishing Treatment Relations with Alcoholics," *Journal of Nervous and Mental Diseases,* 134:395-409, 1962. Prior to the initiation of the new approach, very few of the patients referred from the emergency services of the general hospital ever appeared at the alcoholism clinic, and none of those appearing remained in treatment for as long as five sessions. The almost universally held belief was that the kinds of patients receiving assistance at the emergency service were not "sufficiently motivated" to make use of the clinic. Under the new arrangement, members of the alcoholism clinic staff were assigned to the emergency service to make contact with patients. This increased the percentage of patients appearing for a later interview at the clinic to 65 per cent and the number staying for at least five visits to 42 per cent. A similar experiment, to improve the utilization of alcoholism clinic services by women released from a correctional institution, has also recently been reported: H. W. Demone, "Experiments in Referral to Alcoholism Clinics," *Quarterly Journal of Studies on Alcohol,* 24:495-502, 1963. See also H. J. R. Koumans and J. J. Muller, "Use of Letters To Increase Motivation for Treatment in Alcoholics," *Psychological Reports,* 16:1152-4, 1965.

The necessity of overcoming excessive reliance on certain types of therapeutic approach is not, of course, restricted to alcoholism clinics; it applies equally to general psychiatric agencies and to many other helping services. If mental health centers are to live up to their expectations as true community agencies, they will have to modify and expand the approaches used in the past by most psychiatric clinics and mental hospitals.

TRANSITIONAL FACILITIES

Recent years have seen the expansion of *half-way houses* and *recovery homes* for problem drinkers. These transitional facilities attempt to bridge the gap between 24-hour institutional care and independent living in the community. Residents in these facilities are expected to obtain a job as soon as possible and to pay a certain amount weekly for their room and board. The majority of these homes have been developed through the efforts of members of Alcoholics Anonymous, and a much smaller number through the efforts of church organizations and state alcoholism programs.[18] Most of the facilities are small, providing care for less than thirty persons. Half-way houses for women, which are still very rare (except in Southern California), tend to be even smaller.

Although some of these facilities are beginning to work with professional agencies, the only treatment programs in most are A.A. meetings. The staff of the houses gener-

18. An accurate count of the number of such facilities is almost impossible because some are always closing and new ones opening and also because it is difficult to know what criteria to use for inclusion. There are now more than 100 half-way houses in the United States, with the greatest concentration in the Los Angeles area: 30 half-way houses, including some with over 50 beds.

ally consist of recovered problem drinkers, who work for very little salary beyond their room and board. The financial situation may be quite precarious. Despite the name, residents of most half-way houses come directly from the community rather than from a mental hospital or correctional institution. There are strict rules about abstinence in the homes. Admission and discharge policy is generally in the hands of the resident manager. The residents usually are not Skid Row men, but they often have very uneven employment histories and most are separated from their families.

The future of half-way houses and other types of intermediate facilities is uncertain. They have arisen to fill a void in community services for problem drinkers. Existing and future half-way houses need to establish better relations with other helping agencies and a sounder financial basis for their operation.

Day and *night hospitals* are gradually being developed in association with other psychiatric services in the United States. A day hospital provides treatment for patients in need of intensive psychiatric care who are unable to manage on their own during daytime hours and cannot hold a job, but who are able to return to their families at night. Night hospitals provide similar services for those patients who work or attend school during the day, but who need support in the evenings. Many problem drinkers could use such services, but the small number of such hospitals presently in existence cannot provide care for these patients. A few alcoholism units of mental hospitals in metropolitan areas do function as night hospitals on an informal basis. The services of day and night hospital units in community mental health programs should be made available to all problem drinkers.

COMPARISON OF PSYCHOLOGICAL APPROACHES USED WITH PROBLEM DRINKERS AND IN GENERAL PSYCHOTHERAPY

There are some differences between the psychological approaches generally used in the treatment of problem drinkers and those used with general psychiatric patients. On the whole, therapists working with problem drinkers tend to deal more actively with patients than do therapists in general psychiatric facilities. Often they directly confront the patient with his drinking problem; however, this is done in the context of a previously established relationship, and care is taken not to reject the patient in any way.

Therapists in alcoholism facilities frequently stress the immediate situation of the patient; that is, they try to assist him to understand better his reaction to various stresses and to cope more adequately with depression and other painful emotions that often bring about drinking episodes. Many therapists are also aware of the importance of unconscious processes but do not pursue work at this level with the majority of their patients.

Group therapy is widely used in special alcoholism facilities, probably to a greater extent than in general psychiatric facilities. The shortage of trained personnel is one major reason for this. Groups frequently deal with denial of drinking problems and attempt to develop group support for a particular type of anti-alcohol or abstinence-oriented set of values. The seeming inability of many problem drinkers to sustain one-to-one psychotherapy is another reason for emphasis on group methods. The role of patients as co-therapists is often stressed, but the professional leader generally retains control. It is felt that the social factors involved in the disorder can best be countered by heavy emphasis on social aspects in the therapeutic process.

A final difference is found in the strong emphasis placed on the drinking behavior itself in most alcoholism treatment facilities—in mental hospital units, special hospitals, alcoholism clinics, and half-way houses. Even if the drinking is viewed primarily as a "symptom," it is still handled differently than are the symptoms of most psychological disorders. Many therapists continuously keep before the patient the fact that he is in difficulty and receiving treatment because of his problem with alcohol. This focus on destructive or damaging behavior is not unique to therapists in alcoholism treatment facilities, however. Psychiatric specialists who work with delinquents, with sexual deviants, with suicidal individuals, or with accident-prone persons generally also pay a great deal of attention to these "symptoms" in their psychotherapeutic work. Many of the differences cited, then, are only in degree, and all psychotherapeutic approaches used with problem drinkers are used with some other general psychiatric patients.

It must be emphasized that the kinds of services for problem drinkers described in this chapter are found in only a minority of American communities. They are by no means as widespread as services for emotionally disturbed individuals, which generally are held to be grossly insufficient in number. The gap between existing services for problem drinkers and the need for such services is, then, great. To overcome this gap will require a substantial investment of personnel and money.

4

Proposals for improving alcoholism treatment services

All agencies should provide services to problem drinkers on an equal basis with other clients

The discrimination of many helping agencies against problem drinkers must be overcome. These patients should have the same access to care that is routinely provided others who need help. Currently, problem drinkers are often treated as second-class citizens, are excluded, or given poor care, by many health and welfare agencies. Medical facilities, psychiatric agencies, social work and welfare departments, rehabilitation agencies, and physicians in private practice should eliminate the barriers—formal as well as informal—against the acceptance of problem drinkers on an equal basis with other patients and clients.

Such changes in the practices of general helping agencies are particularly important because the bulk of the care and treatment needed by problem drinkers can be provided by these agencies. In the development of services for these patients, there should be an awareness of the numerous other problems accompanying the drinking problem. Problem drinkers may be hungry or severely obese, poor and jobless, diabetic, or psychotic. Much of the care and treatment required is identical or very similar to that provided for people with other health and behavioral problems.

All opportunities for the establishment, expansion, and improvement of services should be utilized

The social, psychological, and physiological variability of problem drinkers imposes a need for many different kinds of treatment and intervention for their rehabilitation. Major factors relating to the appropriateness of different treatment approaches are: the nature of the patient's drinking, his physical health, his psychological characteristics, and his social circumstances.

Services for problem drinkers should be developed within *traditional helping systems*—public-health, mental health, general hospitals, public-welfare, vocational rehabilitation, medical practice, and so on. Services for problem drinkers should be developed as parts of *newer efforts* to cope with health and welfare problems, such as the economic opportunity and urban development programs. Community service centers, for example, should provide assistance to problem drinkers.

Additional personnel and funds should be provided to ensure appropriate services by all agencies

Special attention will have to be devoted to problem drinkers until satisfactory care is available for them, either through special programs or through the existing structure of helping agencies. Various approaches may be utilized to effect the desired changes within agencies and institutions. One means is the addition of special alcoholism personnel to the principal helping agencies to function as "catalysts," coordinators, and consultants, and to assist the local staff. A key responsibility of these specialists would be to make sure that the treatment needs of problem drinkers are considered in all planning, program development, and day-to-day activities of various departments and agencies. Another means is to set up the guidelines and regulations for governmental funds so as to encourage agencies to give care and treatment to problem drinkers. A third approach is to make additional funds available to general helping agencies if they provide assistance to problem drinkers. All such measures would be temporary, until problem drinkers are accepted for treatment by these agencies on an equal basis with other patients and clients. Where specialized services are developed, they should be closely tied in with the general health and welfare programs. These specialized services generally cannot provide total care to problem drinkers; however, they can often fill especially useful functions in demonstration, training, and research.

Assistance for medical care should be made available

There is an urgent need for communities to improve their medical care for problem drinkers. All *emergency health services*—medical as well as psychiatric—should be available to treat the complications of excessive drinking on the same basis as other medical problems. Similiarly, physicians in private practice should provide assistance comparable to that given to other patients, and home medical care programs and home nursing services through public-health or visiting nurses should be part of a total community program to provide medical care for problem drinkers.

The provision of medical care, when needed, for alcohol intoxication is not treatment of the basic drinking problem. Detoxification treatment or treating the chronic physiological effects should not be confused with dealing with the drinking problem itself. Every episode of hospitalization should be used as an occasion to move the patient toward treatment for his drinking problem. This can be done only if hospital personnel are trained for this task and facilities such as inpatient rehabilitation programs and outpatient (clinic) services are available.

At present, the principal inpatient programs are in mental hospitals. As community-based psychiatric services (in general hospitals and mental health centers) are expanded, they should provide care for many types of patients now admitted to alcoholism units in mental hospitals. While some psychiatric facilities can develop special programs for problem drinkers, few will likely be in a position to set up separate wards for them. However, these patients should receive the same quality of care as other psychiatric patients. The treatment programs should be flexible and responsive to the varying needs of different patients. In addition, outpatient follow-up care should be arranged for all patients.

Where special treatment and rehabilitation services exist for problem drinkers, they should have close links with community mental health programs, medical facilities caring for intoxicated persons, and other community agencies, such as clinics and half-way houses.

Long-term inpatient care may be required for severely handicapped problem drinkers unable to function adequately in the community. While many of the traditional rehabilitation and treatment methods may not be appropriate, the emphasis should still be on improving the patient's ability to manage his own life. Facilities of this type will, in most cases, also serve those with other kinds of problems, and will probably accept and release patients on a voluntary basis.

The majority of problem drinkers do not require the services of either inpatient treatment centers or intermediate facilities. *Out-patient* (or *clinic*) *care* is the basic form of assistance for them. This could be supplied through community mental health programs or as part of the general services of psychiatric clinics. Some community mental health centers may have a special program for these patients; others may provide clinic treatment as part of the general psychiatric services. In communities where there are sufficient numbers of problem drinkers, special alcoholism clinics can be a major resource. Where clinics for problem drinkers are administratively separate from other mental health services, care should be taken to ensure that these clinics are not isolated from the other agencies, especially inpatient and intermediate psychiatric facilities. Mental health clinics in general hospitals are in a particularly advantageous position to receive patients from the medical emergency services.

Too often hospital treatment goes for naught because of the absence of arrangements for continued treatment when the patient returns to the community. It is not enough to plan for this continuity on a case-by-case basis. Administrative agreements between agencies regarding the transfer of cases are also needed. Clinic personnel should make contact with patients (and their families) prior to discharge from the inpatient facilities.

Intermediate (or transitional) facilities should be available as parts of all community treatment programs

Partial hospitalization, recovery homes (or half-way houses), and residential home placements are key elements in a total community program of care and assistance for problem drinkers. The development of this type of intermediate service is still in a rudimentary state, but its utility has been demonstrated. Such facilities often serve as alternatives to hospitalization and in other instances they can function as necessary bridges between total institutional care and independent living in the community. Although such facilities may be physically separate from other helping programs, it is essential that they be closely tied to inpatient and outpatient services. Since some of the smaller recovery homes may have little or no professional staff of their own, arrangements should be made to provide treatment and rehabilitation services. Because of the relative novelty of intermediate facilities, especially half-way houses and recovery homes, experimentation with various models and administrative arrangements should be encouraged. State and local tax funds should be made available to support these facilities or payment made on a per-patient basis by the appropriate public agency.

A variety of treatment approaches and settings should be used

Clinics as well as inpatient and intermediate types of treatment facilities should utilize many different kinds of treatment, relying on assessments of individual needs and avoiding the ideological rigidity that still persists in the treatment of problem drinkers. The experimental and innovative approaches currently being used in some psychiatric clinics and hospitals should be tried with these patients also.

One of the major ways in which problem drinkers differ as individuals is in their social-class membership. Social class is a major determinant of values, of expectations, and of feelings about seeking and obtaining help, and so on. Different orientations, therapeutic approaches, and treatment goals are probably required for patients from different social strata. Few clinics, transitional facilities, or hospital programs are able to serve patients from such a wide range of backgrounds; furthermore, patients do not feel comfortable in "mixed" settings. Appropriate and adequate settings should therefore be available for all types of patients.

Alcoholics Anonymous is a valuable resource that can be used in conjunction with many of the programs described above, but the provision of care and treatment to problem drinkers is a responsibility of many professional workers and agencies; the presence of A.A. should not be an excuse to shirk this responsibility. On the other hand, the unusual organizational character and style of Alcoholics Anonymous and of Al-Anon (a companion organization, consisting of husbands and wives of problem drinkers) should not keep physicians, social workers, psychologists, nurses, and other professional persons from encouraging patients to seek help from A.A. whenever it seems appropriate. In this field there is clearly a place for the significant type of mutual aid provided by Alcoholics Anonymous, or by other forms of self-help groups.

Community mental health programs should provide care and treatment

Community mental health programs represent a revolution in the organization of psychiatric services. Not only is emphasis placed on provision, at the community level, of various types of care—inpatient, outpatient, partial hospitalization, and so on—but stress is placed on the use of all care-givers in treatment programs, and on the application of many varied therapeutic approaches to increase the numbers reached by psychiatric services.

Prevention as well as treatment will be a major activity. Located in the patient's own environment and community, these programs will make possible a better understanding of his needs and a more cordial atmosphere for recovery and improved continuity of treatment. As the patient's needs change, he can be transferred without delay or difficulty to other services—for diagnosis, treatment, and for rehabilitation—without the necessity of moving from one community to another. The community programs will accelerate the integration of mental health care with other types of health and social services in the community. The separation of psychiatric help from other agencies can be overcome through new programs like these because community mental health programs will not involve merely one facility or center; they will include a network of separate but related services.

The range of services envisioned as part of community mental health programs is virtually identical with that required for problem drinkers; particularly important is the stress on coordination of major treatment services with other types of community-based services. The treatment of many, if not most problem drinkers, requires the participation of persons trained in social and psychological areas; the greatest number of these will be involved in the community mental health programs. Since it is expected that community mental health programs will deal not only with the mentally ill, but also with a broad range of psychological and behavioral problems among various groups, it is logical that the care and treatment of problem drinkers be included in the work of these programs.

Federal and state support of the programs should be based on the condition that services be provided equally to all patients, and, at least during an interim period, funds should be made available for special personnel to assist in developing appropriate services for problem drinkers.

The case-finding and referral functions of all helping agencies should be strengthened

Many problem drinkers are in contact with general hospitals, psychiatric clinics, social agencies, and welfare departments, but are not recognized as such by the workers in these agencies. The basic training of professional workers and the various in-service programs should include information on the recognition of problem drinkers. Properly trained care-givers among police, judges, clergymen, lawyers, rehabilitation counselors, and probation, parole, and correctional workers, are in contact with large numbers of problem drinkers. They can directly assist these people and their families, and through referrals can participate with the personnel of other agencies in a total treatment program for the patient.

Today the vast majority of such referrals are not successful, in that the person never becomes a patient or client of the agency to which he is referred. Giving a man or woman the name and address of a facility does not constitute adequate referral. Often, in the past, when patients did not follow through on referrals, it was attributed to their lack of motivation; but there is now an increasing realization that motivation is not an "all-or-none" matter and that it can be influenced.[1] Consultation should be available to assist "line" workers in being more effective as referral agents.

Agencies should improve their recording and record-keeping systems

Better recording and record-keeping by agency administrators and staff, and by various government and other officials are urgently needed (1) to improve collaboration and referral between treatment agencies; (2) to make possible evaluative studies; (3) to obtain additional information for planning purposes; and (4) to make possible a wide range of research studies. It is no accident that statistics and records in this field are particularly inadequate; it reflects the strong tendency to minimize, gloss over, and misidentify a wide variety of alcohol problems.

Vastly improved information on patients, on the numbers of people with various kinds of drinking problems, the costs to the community, and related topics is needed to improve the planning, expansion, and evaluation of treatment programs. In addition, such data are essential as background information for assessing the impact of preventive programs.

1. See above p. 80 ff for a discussion of the question of motivation.

Medical and hospital care should be covered by insurance

The financial barriers that often impede the hospitalization of problem drinkers should be removed. These include the present policies of private insurance companies, Blue Cross and Blue Shield, public-welfare programs, and federally supported or subsidized medical care programs that often exclude such patients from hospital and medical care plans.

Industry and unions should develop policies for detection, referral, and treatment

The vast majority of the adult male population—and an increasing proportion of women—are working on a full-time basis. It has been estimated that at least 2 to 3 per cent of the work force are problem drinkers.[2] Often the drinking problems of these persons interfere substantially with their job effectiveness and lead to countless hours or days of work lost due to illness and absenteeism.

Most industrial establishments have been reluctant to initiate efforts because of the fear that acknowledgement of drinking problems among employees may create bad "public relations."[3] In addition, supervisory and other personnel often conceal information because of understand-

2. H. Trice, "Identifying the Problem Drinkers on the Job," *Personnel* (Publication of the American Management Association), 33:527-33, 1957.
3. For a discussion of this and other issues in relation to industrial programs, see A. H. Dana, "Problem Drinking in Industry," *Research Report in Social Science*, Vol. 6, No. 1, Florida State University, Institute for Social Research, 1963, and *A Basic Outline for a Company Program on Alcoholism*, The Christopher D. Smithers Foundation, Inc. (New York, undated).

able concern on their part that the employee may be subject to punitive action, such as suspension, dismissal, or loss of benefits, if his drinking problem becomes known. A number of companies have established definite policies which encourage supervisors to refer problem-drinking employees to the medical department for diagnosis and referral, and they usually specify the conditions under which disciplinary action will be taken. It is usually not taken if the man actively seeks help, and rarely occurs without prior warnings to the man once his drinking problem has become known. Traditionally, employers and supervisors have avoided intruding into the personal lives of employees. Thus, considerable educational work and changes in attitude are required before such company policies become widespread.

Probably close to 50 per cent of all problem drinkers in America are currently employed[4] and consequently industry is an unequalled setting for early case-finding.[5] Information about drinking problems and about sources of help should be made available to all employees by both management and labor unions. In addition supervisory personnel should be trained to help employees recognize they are having difficulty with alcohol, and help them seek assistance from resources both within and outside the company.

4. This figure was used by the Alcoholism and Drug Addiction Research Foundation of Ontario in its proposal for a ten-year plan to control alcoholism in the province.

5. These observations regarding "industrial" programs apply equally, of course, to other major employers, such as government agencies and the armed forces; in fact, there are probably more punitive attitudes present in the armed forces, where retirement benefits are jeopardized for "misconduct" associated with problem drinking. The result is frequently concealment and denial of problem drinking.

It is unlikely that many firms can develop their own alcoholism treatment programs. Only the very largest employers can offer the broad range of medical and social services needed by persons with drinking problems and by their families. The establishment of adequate counseling and referral services is, however, within the capacity of many employers. In-service educational programs are needed because personnel of companies rarely have adequate information on this topic. In addition, the key staff members of medical and personnel departments may also require special training. The task of creating a different attitude toward problem drinkers is certainly no easier in an industrial setting than in the larger society; rejection and concealment operate here perhaps to an even greater extent because of the premium placed on competence and efficiency in work situations.

Organizational mechanisms should be developed and personnel assigned to ensure coordination of various treatment programs

Because the care and treatment of problem drinkers will come from many different agencies, these scattered activities must be coordinated to ensure needed continuity of care and cooperation. This coordination requires full-time trained persons at state and local levels and within certain agencies. An overview of community services for problem drinkers must be maintained so that gaps can be noted and overcome.

Increasing concern to improve the planning of all health and welfare services is evident in efforts already under way to replace piecemeal approaches with more comprehensive ones. The historical tendency to develop programs along categorical lines—as in special programs for crippled children, venereal diseases, mental illness, and the blind—has often resulted in isolated and uncoordinated services, with large segments of the population neglected. The current trend—to develop broad health and welfare programs to meet the multiple needs in any population[6]—is consistent with a major recommendation of this report: that most of the care and treatment of problem drinkers be provided by the general helping agencies, especially mental health, medical care, public-health, vocational rehabilitation, and social welfare.

This trend toward comprehensive health services is important. But many alcoholism workers are gravely concerned that little or no attention will be given to drinking problems under the new non-categorical approach in the health field. This is a danger that should be acknowledged and averted.

At the state level, the coordination of services for problem drinkers can be strengthened through the establishment of special advisory bodies which will periodically bring together all the key state departments. In addition, coordination must be accomplished on a day-to-day basis by a staff given this responsibility. In many states, continuing coordination and planning can be handled by state alcoholism programs.

Coordination at the community (local) level is also of paramount importance. The organizational base for such coordinating activities will vary: it may be provided through community mental health centers, local public-health agencies, health and welfare planning councils, spe-

6. This approach is emphasized in recent federal health legislation—Comprehensive Health Planning and Public Health Service Amendments of 1966 (PL 89-749).

cial personnel attached to local government, or local alcoholism councils.[7]

Additional research should be undertaken in key settings

Additional knowledge regarding almost all aspects of alcohol and drinking is urgently required. Too often, action is guided by myths or strongly held beliefs, or by differing conceptions of "common sense." Only a substantial expansion of research can lead to the knowledge needed. The long neglect of this field in general, and of alcohol research in particular, should be overcome. Very few scientists have investigated aspects of alcohol problems.

Research activities in this field can also have an important impact on the training and recruitment of key personnel. Research in general is currently a central element of training in various fields, including medicine, psychiatry, sociology, and psychology, and research on alcohol problems would signify to those in training the importance of the area and the necessity for various professions and disciplines to be concerned about it.

Clinical studies, psychological as well as metabolic, can add greatly to our knowledge of various aspects of problem drinking. Applied research—including clinical investigations and evaluative studies—is also essential. Studies of problem drinkers are particularly important because some therapists tend to apply newly found treatment methods and techniques on a large-scale basis before the methods have been carefully tested and evaluated. Little is known about the relative effectiveness of various treatment methods for different types of problem drinkers. Which factors

7. Alcoholism councils represent the voluntary (citizens') movement in the field of alcoholism. See p. 181 for a discussion of their role.

are associated with "recovery" and which are associated with "failure"? Particularly informative, also, would be studies of individuals who have overcome their long-time drinking problems without assistance from any profession, agency, or from Alcoholics Anonymous. Much could be learned from the study of a series of "spontaneous recoveries." Investigations in other areas can yield much knowledge relevant to alcohol problems; biological, psychological, sociological, medical, and psychiatric investigations of alcohol use and abuse should become part of studies in general research fields.

Alcohol research should be undertaken in settings where it can have the *maximum* impact on other scientific and professional workers. Studies conducted in key research, training, and service settings could take advantage of the research opportunities and trained personnel in those settings and help overcome the long-standing neglect of this area. Universities, with their basic science departments and professional training schools, are most appropriate settings for investigations of alcohol use and abuse. A federally supported research training program involving doctoral candidates in the psychological and social sciences appears to be highly successful in developing interest in alcohol problems among behavioral scientists.[8] Science departments and the training institutions are in a unique position to interest young professionals in work related to alcohol problems. Closely related to the professional training schools are various agencies and institutions where students can obtain field experiences, such as general hospitals, social and public-health agencies, public schools, jails, and police departments.

8. See E. Blacker, "A Training Program for Behavioral Sciences," paper presented at the Fifteenth Annual Meeting of the North American Association of Alcoholism Programs, September 30, 1964, Portland, Oregon.

Long-term support should be provided to special research centers

Centers undertaking research on various alcohol problems should be parts of universities or of general research institutes and should bring together investigators from a variety of disciplines. Two of their significant roles would be the training of other investigators at the same university and the provision of short-term learning experiences for scientists from other institutions. Some centers could cover areas other than alcohol problems; for example, alcohol-related research can be conducted in conjunction with studies of drug dependence, or as part of general investigations of medical or social problems. There are advantages to having a broad base for a research center: a wider range of personnel from various disciplines is likely to participate, and the interconnectedness of alcohol problems and other problems can be more readily exploited.

A federal grant program should be established to expand research and communication of research findings

A federal research grant program should cover basic and applied studies in this field. Preference probably should be given to investigators who conduct studies in major research, training, or service settings. This would increase the overall impact of grants on other investigators, as well as on educational institutions and program personnel. A specific proportion of the grant funds should be set aside to train research workers. These funds could be used both to ensure attention to alcohol problems in the basic training of scientists and to support a limited number of special training programs in key educational institutions. Finally, long-term (possibly career) support should be provided for well-qualified investigators who show promise of making sufficient research contributions bearing on problem drinking and other alcohol problems.

The availability of funds for research related to alcohol is not likely in and of itself to ensure that the best-qualified investigators will undertake such studies. It is important that well-established senior scientists from various disciplines develop an interest in alcohol-related research. This would increase the probability of significant results from the research and—equally important—would greatly facilitate the recruitment of other scientists to work on these problems. Thus major steps would have to be taken to increase alcohol research by scientists. During the initial period of the grant program the federal personnel involved may actively need to seek out senior scientists and arouse their interest in research on alcohol problems. However, the current research of many investigators is not far removed from alcohol-related issues; showing such scientists the connections between their current research and work on alcohol problems would be one of the primary tasks of grant-program personnel.

Because of rapidly increasing knowledge it is difficult for investigators to keep up with the flow of information in many scientific fields. Fortunately, the bibliographic and information-exchange services for alcohol research are far better than for most other areas.. *The Quarterly Journal of Alcohol Studies* and the *Classified Abstract Archive of the Alcohol Literature* (both prepared and published at the Rutgers Center of Alcohol Studies) provide investigators and others with comprehensive and up-to-date information. However, mainly because of lack of funds, these special resources are not being adequately used. The *Classified Abstract Archive of the Alcohol Literature* is currently available in only thirty-one American libraries. Federal grants could be used to increase the number of medical and research facilities that have these important informational resources. One element in broadening the base of interest in alcohol research is to expand the potential audience for the findings of such studies. This can be done through publications in the general scientific and professional journals, and through presentation of papers at scientific meetings in various fields.

Training programs of all helping professions should include attention to drinking problems

The bulk of the training of personnel in this area should be provided by the basic professional schools. Most assistance for problem drinkers will need to be provided by personnel from the basic helping professions. The creation of a large corps of specialists is neither possible nor desirable. Such a step might lead to even greater disregard of the needs of problem drinkers by the basic care-giving institutions and might also strengthen the belief that these patients are strikingly different and more difficult to work with than other patients.

While there is a major shortage of qualified personnel to provide treatment for problem drinkers, there is also a severe shortage of other kinds of workers in areas such as education, community organization, and consultation. Such workers frequently play key roles in health and welfare planning and program activities and their general lack of background in relation to problem drinkers has further contributed to the neglect of this problem area.

Personnel should be so trained that they are given an understanding of the complex and ambivalent attitudes on all aspects of alcohol use (and non-use) in America, as well as an understanding of the variety of problem drinkers, their particular needs, and various treatment approaches. Knowledge about American attitudes on alcohol use and alcohol problems is essential for developing programs, for dealing with resistance among professional personnel, and for coping with the public's complex reactions to all kinds of alcohol-related behavior. A core element of the preparation for therapists is, of course, supervised clinical experience in working with problem drinkers.

Information on the treatment and medical management of problem drinking should be included at several levels of medical training—classroom instruction, clerkships, internships, and related residency training programs. The treatment of alcohol intoxication needs to be part of the supervised clinical experience of every medical student. This learning should occur in settings which do not perpetuate the attitudes of revulsion and therapeutic pessimism toward drinkers that now generally characterize the educational experience of medical students. Psychiatric training should not be restricted to the provision of detoxification care in emergency psychiatric services, and should include supervised psychotherapeutic work with patients directed at the problem drinking itself.

Social workers are the principal providers of psychotherapy and counseling in most mental hospitals and clinics; social work training should include both classroom work and practical field work experience with clients who are problem drinkers. This can be either in a general social or psychiatric agency that provides assistance to these patients, or in a specialized alcoholism treatment facility.

Clinical psychology students should also be afforded the opportunity to become acquainted with problem drinking, both in classroom work and through the availability of clinical experience in internship training and field work.

Programs of continuing education, extension education, and post-graduate training in the fields of medicine, psychiatry, social work, nursing, corrections, and psychology should include material on problem drinking.

There are major shortages of trained personnel in all of the principal helping professions. The gap between the available number of trained persons and the need for such personnel will undoubtedly increase, in line with the continued expansion of various programs: public welfare; Medicare; community mental health centers; the national heart, cancer, and stroke program; and economic opportunity programs. Discussions about personnel shortages in a particular problem area must take into account the general manpower situation.

The shortage is not likely to be overcome by the recruitment and training even of large numbers of additional personnel; other solutions will have to be found. One possibility is a *modification* of the roles of various trained workers. Many jobs currently being performed principally by highly trained persons could be turned over, at least partially, to people with less training. In addition, a far larger proportion of the time and activities of fully trained professionals could be spent in consultative and supervisory work. For example, psychiatrists can provide mental health consultation[9] to general care-givers, such as public-health nurses, welfare workers, and school teachers. To

9. G. Caplan, *Concepts of Mental Health and Consultation*, Children's Bureau Publication No. 373, 1959, U.S. Department of Health, Education, and Welfare, 1959.

deal with manpower problems there will have to be a willingness to experiment with new approaches and to modify the somewhat proprietary attitudes about professional roles that have existed in the past.

From the standpoint of training, such an approach presents at least two different kinds of challenge. The first is the creation of a core of specially trained people skilled in functioning as consultants and supervisors. A man who is an excellent clinician is not necessarily a good consultant, and additional training and experience may be needed before he can be effective in the new role. The second task is that of developing among basic helping professionals, semi-professionals, and non-professionals, the ability to make use of such expert consultative services.

The better utilization of *semi-* and *non-professional workers* is all the more urgent because of the continuing shortage of trained personnel in all the helping professions. There has been a tradition of using non-professional personnel, particularly recovered problem drinkers, in many facilities. These workers can function most effectively in collaboration with professionals if they have had some previous training. Such training should include: (1) orientation to professional approaches to the problems; (2) knowledge about different agencies and their roles; (3) supervised field experience; (4) emphasis on the importance of assessing each patient's needs; and (5) recognition of the potentialities and limitations of non-professional workers. Various professional training institutions have a responsibility to provide this type of training; extension divisions of universities, adult education facilities, and schools of social work are three places where such training could be given. As training opportunities are developed for non-professional mental health workers and for non-professional workers in other fields—such as poverty programs and public welfare—there should be ample opportunities also to train those who are interested in assisting problem drinkers.

Federal grants should be provided for persons seeking training and for professional schools

While the bulk of work related to problem drinking will have to be undertaken by non-specialist personnel in the general helping agencies, there is need for a cadre of broadly trained people to function as consultants, co-ordinators, and "catalysts."[10] Such people would be familiar with many aspects of alcohol problems and also with general trends in the health and welfare field. Their educational background should include work in psychology and sociology, and in addition, they should have special training and experience in such areas as community organization and group dynamics. A federal training grant program is needed to enable persons to obtain specialized training relating to problem drinking and alcohol problems, and to fill out their general background in various related fields. For example, a psychiatric social worker might divide his training time between experience in a facility treating problem drinkers and learning about public-health and sociological concepts he had not previously been exposed to. Or a sociologist might need exposure to general clinical work as well as specific training relating to problem drinking. Those with a broad background in fields of health and welfare and with special experience with problem drinkers would be uniquely qualified to function as "catalysts" to aid personnel of general helping agencies.

10. See p. 177 for a description of the roles of such specialists.

They could also, of course, function in consultative and program-development capacities at various levels of government.

Federal funds are needed to assist in introducing materials on alcohol use and abuse into school curricula. Such funds could be used to support special institutes and workshops for the faculty and also to provide trained supervisors for clinical field work settings. In addition, funds are needed to add full-time (or part-time) personnel with special knowledge and experience in the field to the staffs of professional training schools. Such personnel would be the focal point for teaching about alcohol problems in each school.

Increased attention to the needs of problem drinkers on the part of professional training programs could change the attitudes and practices of care-givers and thereby contribute greatly toward improving treatment. The men and women who are currently being trained will soon constitute the bulk of the persons providing care in American helping agencies; they could, within a relatively short time, introduce major improvements in the services given to those with drinking problems.

5

The special problem of public drunkenness

The traditional handling by the police, the court, and
jail systems of the very large number of persons found
drunk on the streets is inhuman as well as ineffective.
There is general agreement that the current "revolving
door" system of repeated arrests and jailings does not
alter the drinking behavior of any significant number of
problem drinkers, and that it is not effective either as a
deterrent or treatment. Many questions have been and are
being raised about the constitutionality of treating such
persons as criminals. If a man's drunkenness is part of his
illness—and thus a non-voluntary act—he should be treated
as a sick person and not as a criminal.[1] Clearly it is not a

1. In one recent decision, *Driver v. Hinnant*, 356 F.2d 761, the U.S. Fourth
Circuit Court of Appeals ruled that a two-year sentence imposed on Mr.
Driver for public drunkenness was "cruel and unusual punishment." The
court ruled that "the state cannot stamp an unpretending chronic alcoholic as a criminal if his drunken display is involuntary as the result of
disease. However, nothing we have said precludes appropriate detention
of him for treatment and rehabilitation so long as he is not marked a
criminal." In *Easter v. District of Columbia*, 361 F.2d 50, another court
stated that proof of "chronic alcoholism" was a defense against a drunkenness charge because the defendent "has lost the power of self-control in
the use of intoxicating beverages."

crime to suffer from alcoholism, a characteristic of which is the inability to control one's drinking; thus it seems bizarre, inappropriate, and unconstitutional to punish an individual for being intoxicated.

In addition, the present handling of public drunkenness offenders is often demoralizing to the police, judicial, and jail personnel. It is an immense economic drain—in terms of men, time, and space—on these agencies. Furthermore, it seriously undermines the professional character of the work of policemen, judges, district attorneys, and others, and often makes a mockery of the American judicial system. In most courts the average time spent by the judge in the "trial" and sentencing of each public drunkenness offender probably is less than three minutes. This system of handling defendants undoubtedly violates the traditional American conception of "due process of law."

Public drunkenness should be approached as a medical-social rather than as a legal-criminal problem[2]

There is an immediate need to find substitutes for the current legal handling of public drunkenness. Police, judges, and prison officials generally do not view public drunkenness offenders as criminals, but they are trapped in the present system by the absence of any alternatives. Since the public wants intoxicated persons removed from the streets, other means of accomplishing this are needed.

The handling of public intoxication from a community-health perspective would represent a major step forward.

2. The recent report of President Johnson's Crime Commission recommended elimination of all public drunkenness laws. See *The Challenge of Crime in a Free Society* (A Report by the President's Commission on Law Enforcement and Administration of Justice), U.S. Government Printing Office, Washington, D.C., February 1967.

Because many of those arrested need medical attention and assistance for other problems, medical facilities, rather than jails, are the appropriate settings for detoxification and diagnosis. The non-medical problems can best be dealt with by social agencies and public-welfare departments. The police would still have the responsibility for bringing intoxicated persons to care-giving facilities, but the "revolving door" system would be replaced by a more rational approach, including determining whether a man detained by the police can be diagnosed as a "chronic alcoholic." This could influence the ultimate handling of the individual, but in any case the immediate management of detoxification would be in medical hands. Subsequent legal action might be taken in cases where laws have been broken.

The question of mandatory (involuntary) treatment for these individuals, and for other problem drinkers, will probably become a topic of increased discussion. There is a strong trend in psychiatry toward voluntary treatment of virtually all patients, with clinical as well as civil liberties reasons behind this development; however, there may be a small number of problem drinkers for whom some type of mandatory treatment is required. The size of this group will not be known until there has been substantial expansion of services for homeless men and experimentation with a wide range of different voluntary treatment approaches for these patients.

A large proportion of those arrested for public drunkenness are homeless men, and thus the problem must be seen in the context of Skid Row. At the same time it needs to be stressed that the problem of Skid Row is not primarily one of alcoholism. Most of the men living in these areas of the city have never been arrested for intoxication; a significant minority do not even drink regularly.[3]

Some Skid Row men are regularly employed, many work occasionally, and others subsist on pensions or welfare grants. Skid Row is not a unitary culture: there are many groups and strata within it. The men and women living in these areas of American cities have in common their social isolation, that is, they lack significant ties to other persons, particularly relatives.

Because most Skid Row men live culturally outside the larger society, special facilities are probably needed to assist in their medical, social, and psychological problems. Generally speaking, these men do not "fit" into the services of existing helping agencies. Their values and life styles are qualitatively different from those of most other people in need of assistance. For example, Skid Row men are usually not found in the alcoholism wards of mental hospitals, are rarely seen in alcoholism clinics, and usually receive only minimal medical care in the emergency wards of general hospitals. Even public-welfare agencies often are stricter in their policies toward these persons than toward other "disabled" clients. The mentally ill, for example, are frequently accepted by welfare departments for disability assistance,[4] while this form of financial support is generally denied Skid Row men.

3. See D. Bogue, *Skid Row in American Cities* (Chicago: University of Chicago Press, 1963), and T. Caplow, K. A. Lovald, and S. Wallace, *A General Report on the Problem of Relocating the Population of the Lower Loop Redevelopment Area,* Minneapolis Housing and Redevelopment Authority, 1958.

4. "Disability Assistance" is one of the categories under which financial aid is provided to indigent persons through joint federal-state welfare programs.

Public-welfare agencies should take major responsibility for organizing services and providing assistance for Skid Row men and women

State and local welfare agencies should take the lead in establishing and organizing special programs for homeless men and women where they do not already exist. Although many city welfare departments leave the care of Skid Row men and women to voluntary agencies—especially to missions and the Salvation Army—a number, including those in New York and Los Angeles, have begun to provide leadership in this area. It is likely that future leadership will come from the public-welfare departments, or from welfare departments in cooperation with economic opportunity programs, public-health agencies, and urban development activities. The health and social problems of Skid Row individuals are so intertwined with their economic difficulties that public-assistance agencies are logical starting points for developing appropriate helping services.

Welfare departments can also provide the necessary coordination and planning in this area. However, welfare departments and municipalities alone cannot undertake this quite substantial and complicated task. A broad attack on the problems of public drunkenness should involve a direct confrontation with all the problems of the Skid Row areas of American cities. The total elimination of most Skid Rows—or at least a great reduction in the number of people living under such conditions—may be possible now with the full cooperation of numerous agencies and with increased community willingness to tackle basic problems rather than mere symptoms. This objective requires federal funds as a stimulus.

The major services needed for homeless persons are: (1) immediate medical care, probably hospital-based, (2) diagnostic and screening services, (3) overnight shelter care, (4) inexpensive lodgings, (5) daytime shelter and recreational facilities, (6) outpatient medical care, probably hospital-based, (7) psychological and social assistance, (8) vocational training and placement, including training in verbal and reading skills, (9) rehabilitation camps, (10) semi-custodial and custodial facilities, and (11) recovery units—half-way houses and more or less protective settings.

A network of such multi-purpose services would abolish the ineffective police-legal system of handling public drunkenness. Provision of the types of social, economic, and medical assistance mentioned above would probably alter the drinking behavior of many of these persons. It would also likely reduce the magnitude of the problem of public intoxication and would overcome in great measure the callousness and concealment that characterize current social responses to this problem.

The Skid Row population of most American cities is steadily decreasing. Recent efforts to tackle the vast problems of urban areas are likely to accelerate this trend. While Skid Row problem drinkers constitute only a small fraction of all problem drinkers, they are often the most visible element. Elimination, or even a sizeable reduction, of the Skid Row population probably would help to undermine a long-standing public misconception: namely, that the Skid Row "bum" is the typical problem drinker. A change in this area might well lead to a change in attitude toward the majority of problem drinkers.

Other long-neglected and often hidden problems of our society—poverty, racial discrimination, poor housing, and inadequacies of educational systems—are now being given attention. The devastating human, social, and economic costs of deprivation are being brought to the nation's attention, with emphasis on the need to spend large sums of money to bring about appropriate social change. There are specific opportunities in several of the newly developing national programs to attack problems associated with the damaging uses of alcohol. For example, any proposed system of legal reform, especially in the municipal or other "lower level" courts, is immediately confronted with the immense problem of public drunkenness in the same way that urban renewal programs have to deal with Skid Row as an issue; similarly, highway safety programs cannot avoid the problem of drinking drivers if they wish to decrease automobile accidents significantly.

As the general care and treatment for all persons—especially those in lower economic categories and those belonging to minority groups—are improved, they should include care for problem drinkers. Specific steps are required to ensure that problem drinkers are not neglected in new programs such as those under the Economic Opportunity Act and in the recently established federal Department of Housing and Urban Development. The same safeguards are required in public-health, mental health, public-welfare, and medical programs. In these major strides toward social improvement there are unusual opportunities to alter American approaches to the treatment of alcoholism, and these opportunities should be fully utilized.

III

The prevention of problem drinking

1

Introduction

The *Final Report of the Joint Commission on Mental Illness and Health*[1] states that humane treatment and rehabilitation of the mentally ill comprise the great unfinished business of the mental health movement. But it may also be said that the great unfinished business is to do something about the social, psychological, and other circumstances leading to mental illness.[2]

Much the same could be said about problem drinking. Prevention should be a major objective of a national alcohol policy. While treatment may alleviate suffering and help maintain or restore social functioning, only through preventive approaches can rates of alcoholism and other types of problem drinking be substantially lowered.

Although treatment for problem drinkers is essential, it is not in itself prevention; treatment efforts probably cannot even cope with new cases as they arise: problem drink-

1. *Action for Mental Health: Final Report of the Joint Commission on Mental Illness and Health* (New York: Basic Books, Inc., 1961).
2. R. J. Dubos, "An Outsider's View of *Action for Mental Health*," unpublished paper presented at the Annual Meeting of the National Association for Mental Health, Miami, Florida, November 16, 1961.

ers are so numerous that treatment for all would require the efforts of most of the professionally trained physicians, psychiatrists, social workers, nurses, and psychologists in the country. And there is little likelihood that the number of workers in these fields could be sufficiently increased to treat even a large minority of problem drinkers. In California, for instance, according to the best estimate available, providing all problem drinkers with weekly contact with a psychiatrist and once-a-month contact with a social worker would require the full time work of *every* psychiatrist and *every* trained social worker in the United States. If instead of millions of problem drinkers in the United States and Canada there were tens of thousands, it might be possible to visualize a treatment approach that could reach all, or nearly all of them.

Contrary to general belief, there is no evidence that control or eradication of any disease has been accomplished by the approach, procedures, techniques, and activities directed at early diagnosis and treatment of disease in individuals.[3]

Prevention aims at reducing the rates of occurrence of a condition. One major preventive approach is to modify causative factors which affect large numbers of people by action directed at broad causes known or assumed to be operating on the population. In public health the emphasis has traditionally been on immunization and on the elimination of noxious agents in the environment; with problems of chronic illness and behavior disorders, stress is

3. E. G. McGavran, "Facing Reality in Public Health" in *Key Issues in Prevention of Alcoholism,* Division of Behavioral Problems and Drug Control, Pennsylvania Department of Health, Harrisburg, 1963, p. 56. This view does not, however, minimize the importance of early case-finding and treatment, both from humane and research standpoints.

placed instead on changing the social, economic, and cultural circumstances that engender unwanted conditions. While knowledge of the causative chain of events is, of course, desirable, preventive programs can be successful in some degree even in the absence of complete knowledge. A reduction in rates occurs if the chain of causal events is interrupted at some point. The program for prevention of problem drinking can be developed along these lines.

"Specific prevention" refers to activities directed primarily at problem drinking. "Non-specific prevention" refers to activities or intervention directed at other problems, but which may also help to reduce rates of problem drinking. If both approaches are pursued, the reduction in the number of problem drinkers will very likely be greater than if they are used singly.

The first group of recommendations is aimed at changing the drinking practices and attitudes of the general population. These proposals are based on the apparent relationship between the customary drinking patterns in a group and the nature and extent of problem drinking in that group. For example, in the United States lower rates of problem drinking are reported among Italians, Chinese, and Jews than among Frenchmen, Irishmen, and Anglo-Saxons.[4] The differences in these rates appear to be causally related to the drinking "cultures" and the systems of social control of these groups.[5]

A substantial reduction of problem drinking is possible

4. See R. W. Hyde and R. M. Chisholm, "The Relation of Mental Disorder to Race and Nationality," *New England Journal of Medicine*, 231: 612-18, 1944, and *Medical Department of the United States Army*, Vol. IX, "Neuropsychiatry," War Department, Washington, D.C., 1929.
5. See Wilkinson, *op. cit.*

if attitudes toward drinking and drinking patterns are altered. Two interrelated approaches for bringing about such social changes are: (1) to initiate large-scale educational endeavors and public discussion about American patterns of alcohol use, and (2) to change laws, rules, and regulations to assist in achieving these objectives. These approaches, which appear to have the greatest likelihood of reducing alcohol problems, are the principal focus of this part of the report.

The second group of recommendations is non-specific; that is, they are valuable and should be pursued for other reasons besides possibly reducing rates of problem drinking. Since there is general agreement that psychological factors do, in an important way, affect most problem drinking, improvements in the general mental health of the population would likely be accompanied by a reduction in rates of problem drinking. If people can develop better means of coping with psychological stress, they are less likely to rely on maladaptive mechanisms such as excessive drinking.

Numerous suggestions have been made for reducing rates of psychological disorders and improving mental health. Three examples are: (1) improving the quality of family life; (2) providing preventive intervention at times of crisis for individuals and families, by both mental health specialists and other workers; and (3) improving general understanding of the nature of human emotions and of interpersonal relations.

Another preventive approach lies in the creation of a better and more humane society—one in which individuals can realize their potential and which includes ample room for diversity. Such a society might well have fewer problem drinkers. The elimination of poverty, the provision of equal opportunity for all, the establishment of adequate preventive and curative medical services for the total population, the reduction of feelings of alienation, and the strengthening of one's sense of community are goals shared by most Americans. They should be forcefully pursued, for their own sake as well as for their impact on many disorders, including rates of alcoholism and other problem drinking.

The two types of preventive proposals—the specific modification of drinking patterns and the non-specific improved mental health and creation of a better and more humane society—are not incompatible; they can readily be integrated, since the principle underlying altering drinking patterns is consistent with basic mental health principles and with the development of a more satisfactory society.

Something needs to be said about research, in line with the recommendations that follow. Continuing research on the relationship between drinking patterns and problem drinking is essential. Base-line information on rates of problem drinking, as well as on drinking attitudes and behavior, should be obtained so that the effects of various legal, educational, and other approaches can be accurately assessed. Only in this manner can future policy be built on past experience. An avowedly experimental approach is required in relation to the modification of drinking patterns, but unless relevant data are collected by governmental and other agencies, there will be no opportunity to evaluate the effectiveness of the new approaches. Base-line information should be collected prior to the introduction of new programs so that comparisons can be made to assess their effectiveness. In addition to epidemiological data on rates of problem drinking, accurate figures on arrests for public drunkenness, on alcohol-related motor vehicle accidents, and on admissions to general and psychiatric hospitals would also be useful in evaluating the impact of preventive approaches.

Various scientific disciplines should be involved in both the basic and applied research bearing on issues of prevention; for example, activities aimed at changing drinking patterns are far more likely to be effective if they are based on knowledge of how different cultural and social groups transmit drinking practices and norms to each succeeding generation, that is, how young people are introduced to and learn about alcohol. In what ways are attitudes and practices regarding alcohol intertwined with other cultural elements and values? Sociologists, anthropologists, and psychologists are by their training particularly well equipped to undertake such studies. Other studies bearing on prevention of problem drinking through social change can, perhaps, best be undertaken by economists, lawyers, and political scientists.

2

Alteration of drinking patterns

BACKGROUND DISCUSSION AND ASSUMPTIONS

One major approach to the prevention of problem drinking is to change current drinking practices. Such changes may be achieved without impinging upon the freedom of either individual drinkers or abstainers. A policy of both encouraging and discouraging certain types of drinking would leave ample room for individual choice. While it is impossible to foretell whether the proposed changes would lead to an increase or a decrease in the proportion of drinkers, it is likely that they would decrease the number of problem drinkers. Nor can one know whether the total amount of alcohol consumed would be greater or less as a result. The concern is not to promote or prevent the use of alcoholic beverages, but rather to encourage changes that will lead to a reduction in alcohol problems generally.

What are some essential characteristics of drinking among groups with low rates of alcoholism? People of Jewish culture and religious orientation apparently have low rates of problem drinking;[1] the rules about drinking

1. Hyde and Chisholm, *op. cit.; Medical Department of the U.S. Army, op. cit.;* and Snyder, *op. cit.*

are well defined. Although there is social drinking, the moderate use of wine as a regular part of religious observances may color all drinking experiences: the whole family, including young children, participates in this ceremonial use of alcohol. In these situations the drinking is incidental to other elements of the religious observance. While differences between Jewish drinking patterns and those of other groups are probably decreasing as Jews become more assimilated in the general American culture, certain significant attitudes toward drinking still prevail. Drunkenness is strongly disapproved of in traditional Jewish culture; it represents a particular type of loss of control, of personal weakness, that is frowned upon. Since psychiatric illness among Jews is at least as high as among non-Jews of comparable social class and educational levels, the low rates of problem drinking cannot be understood in terms of generally lower frequency of psychological disorders.[2] Thus it is probable that attitudes and practices regarding drinking are responsible for the lower rates of problem drinking.

In contrast, among most American Anglo-Saxon Protestants, there is far less clarity about appropriate and inappropriate uses of alcohol. Even when there is apparent agreement about drinking behavior, it is not usually deeply rooted in the culture, and only rarely is it free from conflicting attitudes. While there are differences between denominations, certain generalizations can be made. Drinking among those Protestants of Northern European descent is not usually associated with another activity; rather, its specific purpose is often "having fun" or "escape." Far from being positively connected with deep-seated cultural and moral values, it is associated with the residual uneasiness about the enjoyment of pleasure, an attitude still wide-

2. *Ibid.*

spread in America. In this group there is no agreement about how to respond to drunkenness; people feel vaguely uncomfortable and guilty about getting drunk, but the absence of clear guidelines is striking. This general ambivalence may help to explain why no satisfactory means have been developed for influencing the ways in which youngsters are introduced to drinking. For some youngsters the first drinking experience is an act of rebellion. It may occur outside the family setting and is likely to be associated with guilt and hostility.[3]

Rates of problem drinking are relatively high among Protestant Americans, who do not, however, have an unusually high rate of psychiatric illness. This suggests that the "customary" drinking patterns may account, at least in part, for the high rate of problem drinking. The same inference may be drawn from findings regarding Irish-Americans. Compared to other Americans of the same social classes, the Irish have higher rates of problem drinking. Traditional Irish drinking patterns differ substantially from Jewish ones: among the Irish there is little association of drinking with important rituals; intoxication is often deliberately sought; and liquor, especially whiskey, is frequently used as a "medicine" for a wide range of ailments, physical and other.[4]

A comparison of Italian and French drinking patterns illustrates some additional differences that may be related to variations in rates of alcoholism in the two cultures (high rates among the French and relatively low rates

3. A. D. Ullman, "The First Drinking Experience of Addictive and 'Normal' Drinkers," *Quarterly Journal of Studies on Alcohol,* 14:181-91, 1953.
4. R. F. Bales, "Attitudes Toward Drinking in the Irish Culture" in D. Pittman and C. Snyder, eds., *Culture and Drinking Patterns* (New York: John Wiley and Sons, 1962), pp. 157-87.

among Italians). In France it is widely believed that a certain amount of alcohol (particularly wine) is necessary for one's health,[5] and in some areas of the country a portion of weekly wages is still paid in the form of wine. Drinking in France occurs in many different situations and at almost any time of the day or night. While there is less tendency for French problem drinkers to go on long binges—as many American problem drinkers do—there are no strong taboos in France against drunkenness. In Italy, on the other hand, most drinking takes place with meals. A 1952 survey showed that only one per cent of Italians drink other than at mealtimes.[6] There is far stronger disapproval of drunkenness in Italy than in France or in the United States. Finally, Italians apply little, if any, pressure on persons to participate in drinking.[7] This, of course, contrasts with the situation both in France and in America, where people feel uncomfortable about refusing a drink that has been offered. These differences between French and Italian drinking practices and attitudes may be major factors accounting for the higher rate of alcoholism among the French.[8] It must be mentioned, however, that in some parts of France there is also a high per-capita consumption of distilled spirits, a type of drinking found less often in Italy.

People brought up in totally abstinent traditions who later take up drinking apparently are more likely to be-

5. H. Bastide, "Une Enquête sur l'opinion publique à l'egard de l'alcoolisme," Population, 9:13-42, 1954.

6. G. Lolli, E. Serianni, G. M. Golder, and P. Luzzatto-Fegiz, Alcohol in Italian Culture (New Haven: Publications Division, Yale Center of Alcohol Studies, and Glencoe, Ill.: Free Press, 1958), p. 72.

7. Ibid.

8. R. Sadoun, G. Lolli, and M. Silverman, Drinking in French Culture (New Brunswick, New Jersey: Publications Division, Rutgers Center of Alcohol Studies, 1965).

come problem drinkers.[9] This may partly reflect the belief of abstinent groups that all drinking is bound to be excessive. In addition, of course, drinking in such subcultures evokes adverse reactions from the group. Neither a disapproving attitude, as held by some Protestant groups, nor an excessively permissive one, as among the French, appears to be effective in preventing alcoholism. Instead, cultural patterns with built-in restrictions and taboos against inappropriate drinking—Italian and Jewish practices, for example—are better as models.

Retrospective studies comparing the early drinking experiences of problem drinkers and non-problem social drinkers support the hypothesis that the nature of one's introduction to drinking may influence one's chances of becoming a problem drinker. In a comparative study of the reports of early drinking experiences, the following differences were noted. The problem drinkers, on the average, began their drinking at a later age and were more likely to report using distilled spirits. They also evidenced a greater relative frequency of becoming intoxicated the first time they drank. Often too, their first drinking experiences took place outside the home and were open (or secret) acts of rebellion against parental authority or standards.[10] Early drinking experiences are probably significant reflections of general attitudes toward the use of alcoholic beverages,

9. See J. Skolnick, "Religious Affiliation and Drinking Behavior," *Quarterly Journal of Studies on Alcohol*, 19:452-70, 1958; also, Wilkinson, *op. cit.*

10. H. W. Demone, "Drinking Attitudes and Practices of Male Adolescents," unpublished doctoral dissertation, Florence Heller School for Advanced Studies in Social Welfare, Brandeis University, 1966; T. Menaker, "Conflicts about Drinking in Alcoholics," unpublished doctoral dissertation, Department of Social Relations, Harvard University, 1965; and R. Sadoun *et al.*, *op. cit.*

and for this reason relate to the development of subsequent drinking problems.

Although there is much variation in the drinking patterns of various groups, one may speak of general American tendencies. Mention has already been made of ambiguity and disagreement about not drinking at all, and for those who drink, about how much is appropriate on various occasions. Another cause of trouble is the belief that an ability to "hold one's liquor" is a sign of manliness; in many circles heavy drinking is equated with masculinity. This belief encourages the drinking of large amounts of alcohol and promotes drunkenness. Because of this linkage of drinking with masculinity, some adolescents and young men (and perhaps older men as well) choose this readily available and generally approved way of demonstrating to themselves and others that they "really are men."

Much American drinking is of an "escapist" nature,[11] that is, alcohol is used as means of relieving boredom or emptiness, of getting away from authority and restrictions that are considered intolerable, or of overcoming feelings of inadequacy or inferiority. While drinking for such reasons does not necessarily lead to problem drinking, there is the danger that this method of coping with unpleasant feelings and tensions will become more and more important to the exclusion of other and better ways of dealing with these situations. Those who depend heavily on alcohol as a means of managing feelings of discomfort and anxiety are probably vulnerable to the development of subsequent problem drinking.

11. See H. Fallding, "The Source and Burden of Civilization Illustrated in Use of Alcohol," *Quarterly Journal of Studies on Alcohol*, 25:714-24, 1964.

The special place of alcohol in our society compared to other beverages and foods is shown by the maze of rules and regulations that surround its sale and distribution. This system, with its multiple and contradictory objectives, has grown even more complex in the period since Repeal. It works in such a way that most people have a ready source of alcohol when they want it, yet everyone may say that "something is being done" to restrict consumption. Three principal objectives of the present liquor control systems are to: (1) prevent abuses in the liquor business, such as participation by criminal elements, solicitation for prostitution, and other illegal activities in bars, by "policing" the industry, including enforcement of minimum price and "fair trade" laws; (2) produce income for states and the federal government through the sale and taxation of alcohol and through license fees;[12] and (3) promote temperance.

This last objective, while mentioned in almost all state alcoholic beverage statutes, is usually of minimal importance in the day-to-day work of the state authorities. Enforcing laws against the serving of alcoholic beverages to minors and to intoxicated persons is the extent of direct activities related to the idea of "promoting temperance." This report proposes that a major function of liquor control should be to assist in influencing drinking patterns. However, it should be stressed that while rules and regulations

12. For example, in 1962, the total net income received by the sixteen states that operated liquor stores was $229 million. In Pennsylvania the net income from state liquor stores was close to $50 million. In these sixteen "monopoly" states, an additional $127 million was obtained from licenses and permits. See *Compendium of State Government Finances in 1962*, U.S. Department of Commerce, 1962 CG–SF62-No. 21.

regarding alcohol are an important means of changing public practices and attitudes, by themselves they are not likely to have the desired effect.

Since the early years of this century, it has been difficult, if not impossible, partly because of the long-standing "wet-dry" controversy, to have unemotional discussions about various means of regulating the sale of alcoholic beverages.[13] Opinions about the Prohibition "experiment" are very much colored by the particular ideological stand or position of the speaker; for example, those speaking from a temperance viewpoint are likely to point to the early "success" of Prohibition and to blame its failure on inadequate enforcement, while spokesmen for the alcoholic beverage industry, among others, view the Prohibition experience as a total failure, and as convincing evidence that morals cannot be legislated. There are distortions in both positions.

Rates of problem drinking apparently decreased substantially during the early years of Prohibition, although, at least in part, this was a continuation of previous declines. Reported deaths from liver cirrhosis also declined, as did hospitalization for alcoholism. Arrests for public drunkenness were much lower than earlier. But since the

13. It is significant to recall that in the early 19th century, most leaders in the Temperance Movement did not seek total prohibition. Their objective was only to eliminate the drinking of distilled spirits, not to prohibit the sale of beer and wine. In the years just preceding Prohibition, however, the goal was shifted to the banning of all alcoholic beverages. The extreme "drys" became increasingly strong and took advantage of anti-alcohol sentiment in the country. Similarly, until almost the point of repeal in 1932, the "wets" wanted only the return of beer and low-alcohol-content wine. Only at the end did they realize that it was politically possible to have all constitutional restrictions removed. If less extreme positions had been adopted at either time, the current situation in America might now be quite different.

decreases often continued past 1933, the opponents of Prohibition have argued that the laws against the sale of alcohol could not have been a major factor.[14]

Prohibition was experienced as an intolerable abridgement of personal freedom by many Americans. Soon after it began, a large part of the public began to disregard the intent of abolishing drinking, in defiance of the Volstead Act, and the illicit supplying of liquor became a major industry. While the lack of public support for Prohibition was undoubtedly principally responsible for its failure and eventual repeal, it is an oversimplification to state on the basis of this single, poorly defined, and poorly documented experiment, that laws cannot have any effect on attitudes and behavior. Laws, rules, and regulations can play a significant part in bringing about social change if the gap between the law and prevailing attitudes and customs is not too great, that is, if there already is a tendency to move in the direction required by the legal and regulatory system.

Civil rights legislation, for example, has probably influenced attitudes and behavior toward minority groups and, on the whole, in the direction intended by the drafters of the legislation. These laws, in addition to their legally binding quality, have a significant educational impact. Statutes and regulations express and reinforce public attitudes. A carefully thought-out national alcohol policy should utilize the law as one means of reinforcing certain desirable trends in American drinking practices and attitudes and of discouraging others. Research and discussion

14. There is conflicting evidence for a causal relationship between Prohibition and these changes. For a discussion of this and other governmental attempts to influence drinking patterns and to reduce alcohol problems, see Wilkinson, *op. cit.*

should certainly be stimulated concerning alcohol laws suspected of actually creating problems.

TRENDS IN AMERICAN DRINKING PATTERNS

Over the last seventy-five to one hundred years, there have been several major changes in American drinking patterns. One hundred years ago, more alcohol was consumed in the form of distilled spirits than beer and wine combined.[15] Presently beer is the most popular alcoholic beverage. In 1860, distilled spirits accounted for about 75 per cent of the total consumption of absolute alcohol, correcting for the smaller concentration of alcohol in beer and wine; now the figure is just over 40 per cent. Most of the change has come from an increase in beer consumption—which currently accounts for almost 50 per cent of the total, compared with one hundred years ago when the figure was 20 per cent. Wine has risen from 5 to 10 per cent. Per-capita consumption of distilled spirits is only about half of what it was in 1850 and has remained substantially unchanged since the turn of the century.

Another major change has been in the preferred settings for drinking. As recently as fifty years ago, most drinking took place in public places such as bars and saloons; currently, two thirds of all drinking is done in homes and private clubs rather than in bars, night clubs, or restaurants.[16]

15. R. G. McCarthy, ed., *Alcohol Education for Classroom and Community: A Sourcebook for Educators* (New York: McGraw-Hill Book Co., 1964), p. 134.

16. These estimates are based on changes in the relative proportions of package and "by-the-drink" sales, as well as on findings from questionnaire studies. See M. Maxwell, "Drinking Patterns in the State of Washington," *Quarterly Journal of Studies on Alcohol*, 13:219-39, 1952, and H. Whitman, "Our Drinking Habits," *Alcoholism Review and Treatment Digest*, California Division of Alcoholic Rehabilitation, 1960

A recent trend is the greater acceptance of drinking in the presence of women, and their increasing participation. (Nevertheless, the proportion of women who abstain is still far greater than that of men, particularly in lower economic groups.) A pattern of gregarious social drinking is likely to be more restrained than drinking in exclusively male settings because of greater social controls in mixed company.[17]

There has also been some lessening of the wet-dry controversy.[18] As the use of alcoholic beverages has become more widely accepted, some church and temperance groups have become less adamant; increasingly, their stress is on problem drinking and on reducing pressures to drink, rather than on discouraging all drinking and trying to create an alcohol-free society.

Drinking patterns are embedded in a total culture and cannot simply be transplanted from one society to another. It is unrealistic, for example, to think that traditional Italian drinking practices—emphasizing wine and restricting drinking primarily to meals—could suddenly replace current American drinking patterns. On the other hand, the very diversity of drinking patterns may make it easier to bring about changes in the United States than in a more homogeneous society.

From the standpoint of reinforcing drinking practices that may help to reduce alcoholism and other types of problem drinking, the important trends in American drinking patterns that should be supported and acceler-

17. For a further discussion of trends in American drinking patterns see P. Verden, *Alcohol in America* (in preparation for the Cooperative Commission on the Study of Alcoholism). He also presents relevant data from a recent questionnaire study undertaken in Santa Clara County, California.

18. See above, p. 15.

ated are particularly the increased emphasis on gregarious social drinking and the changes in preferred drinking locales. The passage of time since Prohibition and Repeal, the scientific approach to alcohol problems, increased congressional interest, and the reduced controversy about drinking itself are additional elements encouraging the development of more rational attitudes about abstaining and about alcohol use and abuse. The time is now ripe for broad discussion of proposals for a national alcohol policy. The proposals that follow are an effort to stimulate this type of discussion, which could precede the adoption and eventual implementation of such a policy.

PROPOSALS FOR MODIFYING DRINKING PATTERNS

The general goal of these proposals is to discourage harmful types of drinking and harmful attitudes toward drinking, both in terms of immediate consequences and in relation to the subsequent development of problem drinking. Not all drinking is harmful. Alcohol helps some people to relax, to enjoy food more, and to overcome barriers in interpersonal relations.[19] There are, however, some elements in American drinking patterns that apparently increase the likelihood of alcohol problems. Minimizing these and strengthening those that may function as safeguards against the development of such drinking problems is the purpose of these proposals. They do not imply that abstainers should be influenced to drink; rather they pertain to changing patterns of drinking among drinkers.

There is, of course, no certainty that implementation of

19. For a detailed statement of the positive and integrative functions of alcohol see M. Chafetz, *Liquor, the Servant of Man* (New York: Little, Brown and Co., 1965).

such policies would lead to a substantial reduction of problem drinking; yet it is unlikely that they would have any harmful long-run consequences. The major expectancy of such a program is that it will provide the social setting, the knowledge, and the techniques and leadership needed for a direct attack on these problems. This, then, is to begin the process of prevention.

A deliberate effort at social change is proposed. Laws and regulations are but one element of this endeavor. They will have the desired effect only if supported and reinforced by substantial changes in public attitudes.[20] For this reason a variety of educational approaches, especially enlightened public discussion about drinking patterns, is needed. In the absence of such discussion there is little possibility that the desired changes will occur.

The long-standing barrier to recognizing a possible relationship between drinking practices and problem drinking must be broken down. In the years following Repeal there was a strong disinclination to be concerned about individual drinking behavior except in extreme forms. This report maintains that concern with individual drinking practices is a crucial aspect of any national alcohol policy

20. Major changes do occur in public attitudes and behavior in regard to social issues. For example, during the last forty years there have been remarkable changes in attitudes toward birth control. The taboos, secrecy, and guilt that formerly surrounded this topic have been greatly reduced. Many factors were involved in this virtual revolution, including the changing role of women, campaigns against venereal disease, the continuing weakening of 19th-century views, the "Kinsey Reports," a wider availability of birth-control methods, and increased concern about world-wide population problems. The changes in sexual behavior and attitudes were only partly the result of a planned policy or educational campaign. Changes in drinking behavior and in related attitudes are also the result of many forces. A national policy on beverage alcohol can help to initiate change, and to reduce and reinforce certain existing trends and practices.

aimed at reducing problem drinking and dealing with other alcohol problems. The social objective of reducing damaging uses of alcohol, rather than any wish to interfere with private behavior, prompts these proposals.

Four suggestions for changes in American drinking patterns are listed below. Each is discussed in some detail and examples are given of means to achieve the particular objective. The proposals represent an effort to outline some major changes in American drinking patterns. They should be treated as an entity since they are substantially interdependent. A number of the specific suggestions discussed below are feasible and desirable only in the context of the broad general proposals; individually, they would probably be ineffective and some might have undesirable consequences.

Reduce the emotionalism associated with alcoholic beverages

The emotionalism is a product of numerous elements including: (1) continuing disagreement between "drys" and "wets," (2) residues of the Prohibition experience, (3) differences in attitudes toward alcohol between generations, and (4) various symbolic meanings assigned to drinking and abstinence.

A detached examination of drinking practices is difficult because of the widespread sensitivity to the topic of alcoholic beverages.

Drinking, drunkenness, and even abstaining are often objects of humor or joking. This may well conceal substantial uneasiness and discomfort about the topic. Similarly, many different beliefs are associated with alcohol and drinking. Some view alcohol as an almost "magical" help in managing a wide range of unpleasant emotions and experiences; for others, a drink or two enables them to unwind, temporarily put aside their worries and concerns, and feel more comfortable in their relations with others. Many people feel that alcohol increases their appetite for food and enjoyment of meals. The challenge is to prevent such "facilitative" drinking[21] from becoming a means of escape from reality, and from dealing directly with the tensions and anxieties of everyday life. Alcohol has special qualities, but it is not a panacea, and increased awareness of its limitations and possible dangers is needed. The emotionalism and special meanings assigned to drinking increase the possibility of feelings of guilt, conflict, and anxiety becoming associated with the use of alcohol. They make drinking a readily available focus for psychological problems. This is less likely to happen when drinking is not so endowed with confused, hostile, and frequently concealed emotions.

Widespread public discussion about drinking patterns will enable people to obtain a perspective on their own drinking behavior and that of others through a detached and objective examination of current practices and beliefs relating to alcohol. There are many opportunities for such discussions in service clubs, PTA's, health and welfare associations, youth organizations, and church groups. Newspapers, magazines, radio, and television can also provide opportunities for intelligent examination of drinking in America. Information on both current and past practices, beliefs, and attitudes can serve as the starting point for discussions. Comparisons of various religious and ethnic drinking patterns, as well as the history of alcohol use in America, can be included.

21. See Fallding, *op. cit.*

An often cited undesirable characteristic of American drinking patterns is the social pressure to drink or to drink more. This should be reduced, and tolerance for abstaining should be increased, with complete social acceptance of those who choose to abstain or who drink very little. An atmosphere should be created in which people feel genuinely free to "take it or leave it." The responsibility of the host to make available to his guests a choice of refreshments, non-alcoholic as well as alcoholic, needs to be stressed. This would also make the alcohol less special or unusual. Advertising of alcoholic beverages should therefore include reference to such responsibility on the part of the host. The alcoholic beverage industry would be in a less vulnerable position if alcoholism and other types of problem drinking could be reduced; thus, it would be to the ultimate economic advantage of the industry to participate in efforts to change drinking patterns. The meaningless and burdensome restrictions that harass the industry could then be removed. Various sources—newspaper columns, magazine articles, etiquette books, and so on—which seek to inform men and women on the rights and wrongs of entertaining should also discuss this issue. High school, college, and adult-education home economics courses can also include material on drinking that stresses the host's role in relation to serving drinks to his guests.

Alcoholic beverage advertising may have an impact on drinking practices and attitudes. Liquor, wine, and beer advertisements, especially in the mass media, help mould and reinforce public images about drinking. Current customs and rules substantially restrict the nature and form of these advertisements. Most of these restrictions—some self-imposed, others enforced by states and the federal government—stem from a fear of offending "dry" groups rather than from a genuine concern to reduce excessive or damaging uses of alcohol. The distilled spirits (liquor) industry, for example, decided in 1936 to eliminate women from its advertisements and maintained this policy for twenty years. There is a long-standing informal agreement not to advertise liquor on radio or television. Family situations may not be portrayed in newspaper or other liquor advertising, nor, in many states, may persons (especially women) actually be shown drinking. As a result, the drinking situations shown in most advertisements are often unrealistic. Showing natural drinking situations in advertising might help to reduce the special significance currently associated with beverage alcohol and would reinforce other proposed approaches. Drinking should be shown as a type of activity that can add to the enjoyment of other situations without basically altering them. The undesirability and disapproval of excessive drinking should also be both implicit and explicit in liquor, beer, and wine advertising.

In the years since the Second World War, there has been an increase of drinking in gregarious situations and family settings. There is less emphasis on "men only" kinds of drinking, and a significant proportion of drinking now takes place in homes, with both men and women present. Generally, drinking in a family setting is likely to be restrained. The restrictions on advertising that prevent the depiction of many types of drinking situations might very well be removed. Showing a family situation with one or more of the adults drinking alcoholic as well as non-alcoholic beverages at a backyard barbecue or on a beach, if it has any effect, supports social drinking. Showing drinking by "men only" or in situations in which only drinking takes place, if it has some effect, surely emphasizes those aspects which underlie less socially integrated uses of alcohol.

It is not being suggested that there be more advertising, but that advertising stress themes other than those emphasized under present regulations and industry policies. A key aspect of minimizing the emotionalism associated with alcoholic beverages is reducing the pressure to drink and generally making it more acceptable to be an abstainer or abstemious. The objective is not to encourage more drinking, but to make practical and realistic distinctions between appropriate and inappropriate drinking available.

Clarify and emphasize the distinctions between acceptable drinking and unacceptable drinking

One major shortcoming of current American drinking patterns is the absence of agreed-upon norms or rules about which kinds of drinking are socially acceptable. If this situation could be changed, consistent social disapproval of irresponsible drinking could be expressed and various sanctions instituted to reduce the likelihood of its occurrence.[22] The careful spelling out of what constitutes socially acceptable drinking will be far more difficult than reaching agreement on what types of drinking are to be avoided. The absurdity of defining only "bad" drinking is

22. A universally agreed-upon standard for drunkenness probably cannot be established. The emphasis should be on the behavioral consequences of drinking: when the intoxicated person is behaving inappropriately, group disapproval should immediately exert itself. There may also be a limited number of clearly specified situations in which drunkenness should not be prejudged as irresponsible; however, even in these situations, there needs to be a definite understanding about the limitations or "rules of the game."

analogous to teaching a youngster how to drive only by pointing out what *not* to do; yet this clearly ineffective approach has been pursued in virtually all past efforts to alter drinking patterns. Abstainers and "anti-drinkers" cannot develop the guidelines for drinking; such guidelines will have to be set by drinkers themselves.

Drunkenness is a major type of unacceptable drinking behavior. There are two main reasons for seeking to reduce the amount and degree of drunkenness: first, it often leads to antisocial behavior of various kinds as, for example, driving "under the influence." Second, problem drinking, especially that referred to as "uncontrolled drinking," generally develops only with repeated occurrences of drunkenness. In cultural groups where inebriety is strongly censured, it is found rarely and rates of alcoholism are relatively low. Among Jews, Chinese, and Italian-Americans, drinking itself is not prohibited and the proportion of abstainers in all three groups is very low; however, the distinctions between sanctioned and approved drinking are clear-cut, understood by all, and generally accepted.

The trend toward the use of beer and wine, rather than distilled spirits, has been referred to previously. Because of their lower alcohol content (per unit volume), beer and table wines are less likely to lead to drunkenness. Although people can become intoxicated with a table wine or beer, it takes more effort to do so, and this encourages moderation; thus, the use of these beverages in place of others of higher alcoholic content should be encouraged. Barriers to lowering the alcohol content of whiskey, gin, bourbon, and the like, should be removed, making it legal, for example, to label a drink "whiskey" if it is less than 80 proof (this is currently prohibited). As an additional incentive, a further tax advantage could be given to distilled spirits of lower alcohol content. The further development of ready-mixed "highballs" with lower alcohol content should also be encouraged.

Drinking before driving, even when it does not involve drunkenness, entails increased risks of accidents. Effectiveness in many types of activities—especially those involving great skill or dexterity, or the use of judgment—may be impaired by relatively small amounts of alcohol. A far better understanding of the nature of this impaired functioning is needed and would lead to clearer distinctions between acceptable and unacceptable drinking.

Deliberate efforts are needed to develop a greater national consensus regarding approved and disapproved drinking behavior. Widespread educational efforts are required, involving many organizations. A number of existing governmental and voluntary health and welfare agencies—as well as the proposed new national organization[23]—should take the lead in the planning, organization, and execution of a continuing educational campaign stressing the differences between types of drinking. In the absence of such activity there is little possibility that any legal and regulatory changes will be instituted and supported.

There is an analogy between the responsibility of the alcoholic beverage industry and that of the automobile industry. It is now accepted that the motor vehicle manufacturers routinely provide minimum safety equipment on all cars. The combination of automobile and driver—a human being with certain frailties—creates potentially dangerous situations. Similarly, the combination of beverage alcohol and human beings, with their particular psychological and social vulnerabilities, creates potentially harmful situations. A producer has the responsibility of dis-

23. See pp. 167-8.

couraging harmful uses of his product. The advertising of alcoholic beverages regularly ought to include specific reference to the distinction between acceptable and undesirable drinking. An appropriate federal agency[24] could be given the responsibility of working with the alcoholic beverage industry to foster such advertising; should voluntary efforts not achieve the desired results, the agency might then be given additional regulatory powers.

The host at a party also has some responsibility to minimize excessive or irresponsible drinking. Some Scandinavian hosts, for example, make it a practice to find out whether a guest is driving that evening before offering him an alcoholic drink. To develop such attitudes in America will not be easy, since current practice generally requires the host to keep all glasses full and often to push another drink on his guests before they are ready for it. Liquor advertisements, newspaper columns, "style-setting" magazines, and other moulders of the national "etiquette" can all assist in altering the present conception of the host's role and responsibility.

The above are examples of possible ways of clarifying the difference between acceptable and unacceptable drinking. With a few exceptions they are stated in negative terms, that is, they fail to indicate what are the characteristics of acceptable drinking. There have been recent efforts to define these characteristics. For example, "integrative" and "facilitative" drinking are described in terms of the psychological functions and meanings that drinking has for the individual.[25] Such an approach

24. See Wilkinson, *op. cit.*, for detailed proposals regarding a federal alcohol agency to deal with problems of pricing, sale, and advertising.
25. See Fallding, *op. cit.*, and R. Nevitt Sanford, "A Normative Theory of Drinking Patterns" in *Alcohol Problems and Public Policy* (in preparation for the Cooperative Commission on the Study of Alcoholism).

stresses the relation of drinking to the whole personality. Accordingly, if it is consistent with personality growth and development it is "integrative." These efforts still fall short of spelling out what constitutes appropriate drinking in terms of how much is consumed, the accompanying activities, the rates of drinking, and so on. It may be unrealistic to seek specification along these lines, but some further guides are urgently needed. The major challenge remains that of defining drinking in positive terms rather than solely by negative criteria.

In the long run, the success of efforts to curb drunkenness and other forms of destructive behavior depends on the willingness of Americans to express their concern and take appropriate action when such drinking occurs. The present general unwillingness to intervene in such situations springs from the failure to recognize that disapproval of inappropriate drinking is not condemnation of all drinking.

Discourage drinking for its own sake and encourage the integration of drinking with other activities

The nature of Chinese, Jewish, and Italian drinking patterns suggest that drinking alcoholic beverages primarily in association with other activities creates certain safeguards against destructive and dangerous types of drinking. Drunkenness, for example, is usually inappropriate if other activities are going on concurrently; thus the emphasis is on moderation. When drinking becomes an incidental part of routine activities, including those related to leisure time, important barriers are set up against potentially harmful kinds of drinking. By contrast, present customs and regulatory policies often restrict drinking to situations and settings in which the principal focus is on drinking and where, in the absence of other activities, there is, accordingly, a reduction of pressure for moderation. The personal anonymity, darkness, and generally furtive quality of many bars permits and even encourages behavior usually not considered socially acceptable.

Several state liquor control authorities have been issuing an increasing number of licenses to places other than bars, such as bowling alleys, winter resorts, and restaurants. This way of integrating drinking with other activities should be encouraged because the drinking is likely to be guided by the basic rules of conduct of the particular activity or setting, and drinking behavior will generally remain within rather clearly defined limits. Drinking as adornment for other activities, or as part of the celebration of significant events—the signing of contracts, weddings, or the toasting of a winner—carries with it a relatively small hazard. In addition, the desirability of liquor advertisements depicting persons in eating situations is clear. Drinking with meals provides the physiological "buffering" effect of food and the resulting slowing down of alcohol absorption in the body; furthermore, it often takes place in family settings with built-in social controls against excess. Restaurants and beverage advertisers might therefore collaborate in some of their promotional materials; certain food producers might also join with the beer or wine industry in advertising campaigns.

Stressing drinking as an integral part of other activities rather than drinking that is engaged in for its own sake is, of course, closely connected with efforts to reduce the strong feelings surrounding alcohol use and is linked with efforts to clarify acceptable and unacceptable drinking behavior.

Assist young people to adapt themselves realistically to a predominantly "drinking" society

The question of the "learning experiences" of youngsters in relation to beverage alcohol is sufficiently important to merit separate consideration. The present circumstances under which young men and women begin their participation in the larger "drinking culture" are often entirely haphazard. The legal age for the purchase of alcohol is twenty-one in most states, and in a number of states all drinking by minors is a violation of the law.[26] Yet the actual facts about drinking in the under-21 group are very different. Over 75 per cent of high school students report that they have had alcoholic beverages more than once prior to graduation (age 17 to 18), and one third state that they drink with some regularity.[27]

26. In New York and Louisiana, however, all alcoholic beverages may be purchased at 18. In South Carolina, Kansas, Ohio, and West Virginia, the age for purchase of beer is 18; also, in the District of Columbia and Wisconsin, both beer and light wines are available at 18. In North Carolina, married persons may purchase all alcoholic beverages at 17, but unmarried men and women must be 21.

27. There are, of course, regional, religious, and urban-rural differences in relation to rates of teenage drinking. Some other findings from studies of teenage drinking are the following: half of the youngsters reported that they first drank in their own home. Less than half who drank stated that they had a drink the week before being questioned. One third reported that they had been "high" one time or another. Most teenagers who drank never got into trouble because of their drinking. See N. M. Chappel *et al.*, *The Use of Alcohol Beverages Among High School Students* (New York: The Mrs. John B. Sheppard Foundation, 1953); C. Sower, "Teen-Age Drinking in Michigan" (summarized in *Connecticut Review on Alcoholic Beverages Control, New York State Legislature, 1963*, by L. M. Wakoff Research Center and the Staten Island Mental Health Society, Inc.; and G. L. Maddox and B. G. McCall, *Drinking Among Teen-Agers: A Sociological Interpretation of Alcohol Use by High-School Students* (New Brunswick, New Jersey: Publications Division, Rutgers Center of Alcohol Studies, 1965).

The age limit of 21 is currently largely unenforceable. In addition, it creates a basically hypocritical situation reminiscent of the Prohibition era. (In principle, all age restrictions for alcohol probably should be eliminated, but this would probably be too precipitous a change.) Perhaps, during a transitional period, while other changes are occurring in American drinking patterns, a minimum age of 18 for public drinking or purchase might be adopted. Eighteen is the usual age of graduation from high school, many marry at this age, and men are eligible for military service; a few states even permit voting at 18.[28] Finally, it does not appear that teenagers get into more difficulty with alcohol in those states where the legal age for purchase is 18.

Driving cars, smoking, and holding a job are all aspects of adult roles. For many youngsters drinking also represents an effort to assume adult roles. Some adolescents, of course, do drink to "experiment," to see what it feels like, but youthful drinking is often not just a rebellious act; it is also an effort to participate in adult behavior patterns. Social meanings rather than pharmacologic effects are probably the key reason for most teenage drinking.

If the minimum age for the purchase of alcohol were lowered to 18, legal barriers against the use of alcohol on most college campuses would be greatly reduced, since relatively few students are under 18 (and exceptions might be made for those who are). Colleges could permit the serving of beer and wine in student social centers and cafeterias, and alcoholic beverages could also be allowed at dances and other social occasions. College authorities, student organizations, and student government bodies would be responsible for maintaining the distinction between sanctioned drinking and drinking behavior that violates

28. The minimum age for voting is 18 in Kentucky and Georgia. It is 19 in Alaska and 20 in Hawaii.

the rules and norms of the campus. Models for acceptable drinking would have to be established. There should be no pressure to drink, and abstinence should be respected. Drinking by college-age students in settings of this kind, rather than illicitly either on or off campus, would help to place alcohol in a more reasonable, healthier context. Even minimal availability of beer and wine on college campuses might reduce the current hazardous practice of groups of students piling into a car, driving several miles to a bar, drinking substantial amounts of alcohol in settings lacking the desired social controls, and then driving back to the campus. The college years provide an excellent opportunity for students to engage in formal and informal discussions about alcohol use and abuse and to apply their creative intelligence to this problem. If colleges can become places for enlightened learning about alcohol and drinking, considerable progress will have been made toward creating better and less damaging drinking patterns.

Americans prepare for participation in most adult roles; for example, teenagers are not allowed to drive without ample instruction from adults. Yet there is generally no preparation of young men and women for their imminent exposure to a drinking culture where they will be confronted with many decisions about whether or not to drink and how to drink. The present combination of laws, rules, and practices—the last often in violation of existing laws—seems designed deliberately to prevent any sensible preparation of youngsters for responsible participation in the adult society where most drink.

Although schools assume much responsibility for preparing youngsters for various adult roles—vocational, citizen, and familial—the home remains the primary setting for learning social behavior. However, because of ambivalence about alcohol use in America, the teaching and learning opportunities of the home often have not been utilized. Parents should be assisted to be more effective in this area, and material on alcohol education should be as readily available as that on sex education.

In addition to the home, other situations can offer opportunities for young people to learn about alcohol. Since peer groups are very important to most teenagers, some opportunities might be found to introduce alcohol in non-familial settings. In these settings drinking could be integrated with other activities and would not become the center of attention, no pressure would be exerted on young people to drink and the "specialness" of the occasion would be minimized as much as possible. The fact that alcohol is available would be incidental to the primary activity. Alcohol might be made available under these conditions at youth functions such as those organized by church, recreational, or athletic groups. Prohibitions against excessive or inappropriate drinking would then be unambiguous, clearly understood, and effectively enforced. Since these are learning situations, adult supervision would be stressed.

Increased opportunities for more realistic instruction about alcohol use and non-use are needed. Improvements in this regard, aimed at promoting more responsible attitudes toward beverage alcohol, can be achieved only if the issues involved are faced directly and if some time-honored biases and stereotypes are overcome. The hypocrisy which characterizes much of the current manner of dealing with teenage drinking should be eliminated. Better means, formal as well as informal, can be developed for teaching young people about beverage alcohol, but parents need to take major responsibility in the training of youngsters.

Action to reduce the emotionalism associated with alcohol use would be of particular importance in the learning experiences of young people. It would, at least partially, counteract the "forbidden fruit" reaction of many teenagers to beverage alcohol which renders drinking more attractive because it is prohibited (though not very effectively or wholeheartedly) by the older, parent generation and by other authorities.

3

Altering drinking patterns through education in the schools

Alcohol education in schools should be guided by the goals that have already been stated for American drinking patterns. However, effective work toward these goals in schools depends heavily on progress and enlightenment regarding alcohol use in the larger society. Because of their dependence on local support, schools tend to be rather conservative and to follow rather than to lead, especially in non-academic areas. School administrators and most classroom teachers usually stick closely to the expressed values and beliefs of the community in which they are employed.

Although the laws in virtually all states require some instruction on alcohol, the amount of classroom time spent on alcohol education is insignificant and usually ineffective. Classroom teachers, along with the vast majority of Americans, are trapped by the cultural and emotional conflicts surrounding the topic. On the whole they are ill-equipped at present to help their students achieve a better understanding of the issues involved in the use of alcohol. In addition, there is great uncertainty regarding the objectives of alcohol education; for example, should the teacher have as a goal increasing the proportion of abstainers while the students are in high school, and as adults as well? Should she help them distinguish between destructive and non-destructive uses of alcohol; or should her role be restricted to pointing out the dangers of excessive drinking—a problem not likely to be of concern to the vast majority of students? Teachers soon discover that there is little consensus on what constitutes alcohol abuse—perhaps even less than in relation to sexual behavior.

School teachers, probably more than the population at large, tend to be rather anti-alcohol. The proportion of abstainers among unmarried middle-class women (and this is still what many school teachers are) is far higher than for the general adult population or even for all American women. The anti-alcohol emphasis of teaching usually comes through—sometimes explicitly, but often in more subtle form. Also, in most communities, although abstinence is officially approved for adolescents, there is no similar acceptance of appropriate drinking; this immediately undermines any possible effectiveness of alcohol education, since the parents of many of the youngsters drink and many of the youngsters themselves have already experimented with alcohol. Interest and involvement in the topic rapidly disappear when youngsters sense the disparity between what is being taught and what they know to be the reality.

Most teachers are trained to deal with academic material. Taboo or controversial topics are generally avoided in the classroom and teachers usually have had little training or experience in allowing free discussions of controversial issues or in encouraging students to air their feelings. Yet in order for alcohol education to be effective, such discussions must take place. Alcohol education is part of a larger effort to encourage personality growth and foster good mental health. Discussions about drinking can serve as examples of the application of human intelligence and reason to controversial issues and emotionally charged questions—to be sharply distinguished, of course, from discussions for or against drinking or for or against abstinence, a distinction which educational leadership has so far failed to make.

While factual information about the nature of alcohol and its effects on the human body should be made available to youngsters, this alone is not adequate alcohol education. Behavior in relation to alcohol, for young people as well as adults, involves attitudes, values, and feelings. Discussions, if teachers are adequately prepared to handle them, can acquaint young adults with the controversy over drinking in our society; give them some perspective on different drinking and non-drinking practices, including those of their own cultural group; and can inform them about historical facts underlying the current situation. Such discussions, more than facts alone, will help to overcome the emotional "mystique" about alcohol. Because of deep-seated attitudes about alcohol—which do affect young people—the discussion situation, with the opportunity for airing feelings and learning from one another, is the best procedure for alcohol education. Motives for drinking, for excessive drinking, and for abstaining can be explored under the leadership of the classroom teacher. The teacher offers an example, not in terms of whether she personally drinks or not, but in terms of the kinds of attitudes and approaches toward alcohol use that she displays and encourages.

Alcohol education should come in many different parts of the school curriculum. Alcohol use and alcohol problems can be discussed in relation to a great many subjects—chemistry, social studies, English, history, biology, and health education. There are considerable advantages to treating the topic in this way rather than expecting that a single unit or syllabus will do the job; this latter approach may actually reinforce emotionally charged attitudes about this topic. Classroom teachers rather than outside "experts" should handle the areas of alcohol use and alcohol problems. The use of such experts is likely to reinforce views about the specialness of the subject and to increase anxiety in relation to it.

Additional emphasis in the training of teachers should be placed on the psychological dimensions of learning, that is, that maximum intellectual growth cannot take place in the absence of general personal and social development. Teachers should permit and encourage the discussion of controversial questions. The classroom experiences of teachers in training can prepare them for this. Alcohol and drinking are ideal model topics for teacher-training of this kind. The training should sensitize them to the importance of interpersonal relations and non-verbalized feelings in the classroom learning situation. Knowledge from psychology, sociology, and group dynamics should be made an integral part of their training.

Education about alcohol should be an integral part of all driver-education courses

Because driving is of prime importance to high school students, many enroll in driver-education programs, which are available in most parts of the country. Using the topic of drinking and driving as a starting point, much useful education about alcohol could be undertaken in these driver-training courses. Attempts to teach youngsters about the dangers of drunken driving are not likely to succeed without broad discussions of the whole topic of alcohol use in American society; slogans such as "If you drink, don't drive," or showing a movie on accidents rarely have the desired effect. Driver education presents a unique opportunity for exposing youngsters to facts and ideas about alcohol that are probably not included elsewhere in their educational experiences. Unfortunately, driver-education instructors at present are usually not well equipped either by training or experience to be effective in the area of alcohol education. The use of group-discussion methods is rare in driver-education programs and few instructors have had an opportunity to learn how to deal with the topic. All programs to train driver-education instructors should include material and instruction on how to deal with the topic of alcohol in such courses.

Alcohol-education consultants should be attached to the Office of Education

The role of the Office of Education, one of the divisions of the federal Department of Health, Education, and Welfare, has greatly expanded in recent years. It is now in a position to provide assistance to states in a variety of ways. Alcohol-education specialists can be assigned to the Office of Education for functions such as the following: (1) to coordinate and provide leadership for activities within the Office of Education that relate to alcohol education; (2) to encourage and assist state educational authorities (through grants-in-aid or contracts) to work with local school authorities in developing alcohol-education ac-

tivities; (3) to provide funds for demonstration and research projects in relation to alcohol education; and (4)
to provide consultative and other assistance to teacher-
training institutions to ensure appropriate attention to
alcohol education in the curricula of these educational
programs.

Each state education department should assign personnel to work in the area of alcohol education

Alcohol-education specialists are needed to participate in
educational activities aimed at altering attitudes and behavior toward alcohol. Specialists in each state would
work with local school districts on a consultative basis
to assist classroom teachers to be more effective in alcohol
education. Such specialists could (1) develop in-service
training programs for teachers; (2) work on curriculum
issues; (3) assist in the training of student teachers; and
(4) meet on an individual basis with teachers. Their background and training would be in the fields of education,
group dynamics, psychology, sociology, and community
organization; in addition, they would also have special
training in alcohol education, with particular emphasis
on problems of behavior change. Alcohol educators could
be recruited from experienced classroom teachers, health
educators, and those in special education.

Public schools can supplement and reinforce the education and the learning experiences about beverage alcohol
that come from the home. In both settings the emotionalism, secrecy, and hypocrisy that have characterized the
treatment of this subject in the past should be banished. It
is not suggested here that schools teach students to drink,
nor are they being urged to teach students "not to drink";

rather, the schools can and should teach *about* drinking—a very different thing.

Changes in drinking patterns can play a major role in reducing drinking problems. The school and the home are two of the principal places where youngsters acquire their beliefs, attitudes, and standards in relation to drinking and abstinence. Schools can be truly effective in this regard only when they are in a position to discuss freely and come to grips with the topic of beverage alcohol, when relevant information is available, and when teachers are adequately trained. As American attitudes about alcohol gradually change, the public schools can be more active in helping youngsters develop mature and reasonable attitudes about alcohol and drinking. Changes in drinking patterns and attitudes toward the use of alcoholic beverages can reduce rates of problem drinking, and also have a significant effect on other alcohol-related behavior that is harmful or undesirable, such as "driving" under the influence or destructive or inappropriate behavior while drunk. Minimizing such problems as these is an important objective and argument for altering current drinking patterns.

IV

A coordinated national policy
toward alcohol problems

1

Introduction

Problems such as alcoholism, public drunkenness, and disagreement about minimum age laws, while clearly distinct from one another, can be adequately understood or managed only in relation to the total range of alcohol problems. Rigid categorization was typical of past efforts to manage these different alcohol problems. This is strikingly shown in attempts to deal with problem drinking in total isolation from such issues as ethnic variations in drinking, and strongly held attitudes about drunkenness. A "total alcohol program" must give attention to such diverse problems as hospitalization for medical detoxification, policies regarding drunken driving, regulation of hours for the sale of alcoholic beverages, and public school education about alcohol. A total program must establish general objectives. Unless this is done activity in one area may conflict with action in another, and the result will be reduced effectiveness and increased confusion.

Past responses to alcohol problems (with one exception, consisting of the attempt to eliminate the use of beverage alcohol) have been piecemeal—so piecemeal, indeed, that

different responses to alcohol problems, even though occurring at the same time, same place, and often involving
the same people, were almost totally isolated from one
another. These approaches used different languages, proposed different goals, and utilized different means. All too
frequently their programs clashed, and there were bitter
conflicts between them. Examples of such isolation and occasional conflict may be seen in the various roles of alcohol
beverage control boards, state alcoholism commissions, police departments, and public school systems, and in the
disagreements or marked avoidance of responsibility and
concern among church groups, "helping" agencies, the
major private foundations, and the research professions.

The lack of a consensus for a national alcohol policy has
greatly handicapped efforts to cope with alcohol problems.
For example, in some states the revenue obtained from
liquor taxes and from the sale of liquor in state stores is so
great that it creates a feeling of reluctance to do anything
that might reduce alcohol consumption. Educational campaigns against drunken driving may be muted by fear of
arousing general anti-alcohol sentiment and seeming to
increase pressure on states to reduce their involvement in
the "alcohol business." Communities concerned about public drunkenness, particularly in Skid Row areas, rarely try
to reduce the availability of low-cost wine in such areas.
Nor are concerted attempts often made to influence such
elements of Skid Row as the cheap lodging houses, employment agencies catering to unskilled labor, and pawn
shops, which seem to be crucial to the perpetuation of Skid
Row subcultures.

The development and implementation of a "total alcohol
program" will be a difficult task. It will require a more
open attitude to numerous issues surrounding alcohol use

than has prevailed. Discussions will need to be held by many groups and agencies, governmental as well as voluntary, and the fact that some of the groups and agencies needing to plan and work together have had no previous experience with such cooperation will make the development of collaborative activities more difficult. Alcohol problems impinge upon and involve so many elements of contemporary life—medical, religious, political, judicial or legal, and educational—that only a broadly based approach can bring about the needed changes in the whole pattern of American attitudes and practices in relation to alcohol.

2

Proposals for a coordinated approach to alcohol problems

A total change is needed in the climate of opinion regarding alcohol use. A wide variety of methods will therefore be necessary to develop and implement a national policy. The issues involved must be discussed in the press, in magazines, and on radio and television, to arouse interest in bringing about the required changes. To be effective, the various elements of a national alcohol policy will have to be pursued in a coordinated fashion. The different parts and approaches should supplement and reinforce one another; maximum benefits of a new alcohol policy can be achieved if individual proposals and goals are integrated one with another. It is essential that a single organization or group take responsibility for the creation and implementation of a national alcohol policy, and since no governmental or voluntary organization presently exists that can take a leadership role in implementing the proposals for altering American drinking patterns, a new organization is proposed.

A national organization should be established to help bring about changes in American drinking patterns

This organization, perhaps called the "Committee for a National Alcohol Policy," would consist of leaders from numerous fields—government, sports, entertainment, various industries, labor, religion, communications, public relations, medicine, welfare, and education. The cooperation and participation of the alcoholic beverage industry in the educational and regulatory approaches would also be useful. The proposed program outlined here is directed at drinking problems; it is neither pro- nor anti-alcohol.

The organization would be given quasi-governmental status, having a number of its members appointed by the President, and with an annual federal appropriation. It would obtain the bulk of support for its activities from the general public and from special sources, such as foundations, church groups, and the alcoholic beverage industry. Through its prestige it would have a major impact and could recruit national leaders to serve as models, "style-setters," for different kinds of drinking practices that are proposed. A totally new organization is needed because existing ones such as Alcoholics Anonymous, the National Council on Alcoholism, the North American Association of Alcoholism Programs, and various church groups either primarily focus on treatment or necessarily take relatively limited positions in relation to alcohol use. Generally they are concerned only—or primarily—with the final step of stopping or ameliorating pathology, and are only minimally concerned with altering drinking patterns. The Committee could, on the other hand, articulate the scientific and moral bases for a new social policy; it would create support for a new alcohol policy so that rapid governmental action could be obtained to put the policy into effect. The organization would also encourage and itself undertake research studies related to a national alcohol policy.

Other new organizational arrangements are required to develop and implement a "total alcohol program," both because of the complexity and novelty of the collaborative relationships involved. Within the legislative branch of government new committee structures may have to be developed to cut across traditional committee lines. Committees dealing with such diverse topics as agriculture, finance, liquor control, penal institutions, education, highways, public health, and public welfare, all need to be concerned with aspects of alcohol problems. Within the executive branch there are a comparable number of departments and agencies whose activities involve them with alcohol problems. At both federal and state levels the executive branch faces real challenges in establishing effective means of interdepartmental collaboration. In the United States this has never been attempted in relation to alcohol problems, and even in other (probably less complex) areas such cross-departmental coordination has had only limited trial. Even with the most ideal organizational arrangements much depends on the extent to which key personnel understand alcohol problems and are willing to break with traditional narrow approaches. In this regard, public pressure and a change in the total national climate of thinking about alcohol problems is of major importance. The proposed new national organization can play a major role in stimulating the necessary public discussion on alcohol problems.

The federal government should provide leadership and establish an Interdepartmental Committee

Action by the executive branch of the federal government through its many departments and agencies is essential if substantial progress is to be made in dealing with alcohol problems. Not only must the national government play an active role in developing and implementing a national alcohol policy, but federal leadership will be of great symbolic value to the general public, to voluntary organizations, industry, church groups, and so on, as well as to state and local government. Careful, thoughtful, and well-informed action by the federal government is probably the single most important step in creating a better climate for dealing with alcohol problems.

A permanent structure, such as an Interdepartmental Committee, will need to be established within the federal government to ensure appropriate collaboration among the departments and agencies whose work relates to alcohol problems. While problem drinking (including alcoholism) has been seen primarily as the responsibility of the Department of Health, Education, and Welfare, and while this department has usually been the major focus for all federal activities relating to alcohol problems, a comprehensive approach requires participation by numerous other units of the federal government.[1] This report has emphasized that problem drinking cannot be controlled unless the accom-

1. The Internal Revenue Service, for example, collects large amounts of taxes on alcoholic beverages. Federal alcohol taxes amount to close to $4 billion a year. This exceeds the total for federal estate and gift taxes, and for other excise taxes, such as tobacco and gasoline. There are only two larger sources of income to the federal government—individual and corporate income taxes.

panying alcohol problems are also dealt with. These "other alcohol problems" include such issues as unwillingness to examine American drinking patterns, disagreement about what constitutes acceptable and unacceptable drinking behavior, the relation of alcohol use and criminal behavior, drinking and driving, laws and regulations regarding conditions of sale (including hours, minimum age, prices, and so on), the relation between advertising and drinking practices, and the role of drinking in the Skid Row subculture.

Elements of the federal government that should participate in an Interdepartmental Committee include the Departments of Health, Education, and Welfare; Transportation (traffic safety); Agriculture (wine industry); Defense (both because it has more problem drinkers than any other federal agency and because it runs a very large liquor business of its own!); Labor (dealing with problem drinking in work settings); Housing and Urban Development (Skid Row); Treasury (Alcohol and Tobacco Tax Division of the Internal Revenue Service); plus independent agencies, such as the Veterans' Administration, Office of Economic Opportunity, Civil Service Commission, Federal Trade Commission, and the Federal Communications Commission. Initially it may be difficult for these agencies to collaborate because their relationships to alcohol problems are so diverse and because different alcohol problems have, for so long, been viewed in virtually total isolation from one another. Overcoming this isolation and examining each problem in relation to the totality of alcohol problems is a prime initial objective of a national alcohol policy.

Because of the novelty of this approach a Presidential Study Commission (involving all relevant federal agencies) should be appointed to work out basic policies and guidelines. Any planning and coordinating group, such as a study commission or interdepartmental committee on alcohol problems, should have a permanent staff assigned in order to ensure continuity and provide for necessary work between meetings. Such a staff could be supplied by the Department of Health, Education, and Welfare because of its present substantial involvement in the area of alcohol problems.

Leadership should be provided by the federal government to overcome the continuing neglect of the needs of problem drinkers by many state and local general care-giving agencies. Federal funds are needed to strengthen existing programs and to stimulate the growth of new activities by states and localities. Such action will also graphically demonstrate to the country concern about problem drinking and a sense of urgency. While principal responsibility for action in this area probably will fall to the Department of Health, Education, and Welfare, other federal agencies—such as the Department of Housing and Urban Development and the Office of Economic Opportunity—can make major contributions and should be involved in various planning and program activities.

Substantial funds are currently granted to states and communities for programs such as medical care, public health, vocational rehabilitation, mental health, public welfare, economic opportunity, and urban development; and such federally supported programs will probably increase. States and communities should be encouraged to include assistance for problem drinkers in their general helping services. During a transitional period, federal grants may be needed to assist in developing services for problem drinkers as part of state and local health and welfare programs. These grants might be used particularly to hire a small number of special personnel to act as consultants and coordinators operating within the major existing care-giving agencies at state and local levels.

A permanent Intradepartmental Committee should be established within the Department of Health, Education, and Welfare

The participation of many divisions of the Department of Health, Education, and Welfare is required to deal more effectively with problem drinking. An Intradepartmental Committee would be responsible for: (1) developing overall plans; (2) ensuring continuing coordination of all activities relating to problem drinking; (3) examining and evaluating the Department's activities in this area; and (4) assisting the different units and the Secretary in developing and expanding treatment, education, and preventive efforts.

A permanent full-time staff should be assigned to the Secretary or to one of the Assistant Secretaries to facilitate the work of the Committee. Members of the Committee should represent the Department and be in contact with other high-echelon personnel in the government, with key individuals in national organizations, and with leaders at the state level. A National Citizens' Advisory Committee[2] should be established to ensure that the Department has the assistance of top experts in the development and implementation of comprehensive programs for treatment and prevention. This committee, consisting both of persons with experience in alcohol problems and specialists from areas relating to it, would meet regularly to advise the Sec-

2. The appointment of such an advisory committee was announced by President Johnson on October 20, 1966.

retary and the Department. The stature of this advisory committee would also demonstrate the importance that the federal government attaches to action on this issue.

Numerous divisions of the Department of Health, Education, and Welfare should also add new full-time personnel who would be the central focus for alcohol problems and related activities within each division and who would work on a consultative basis with relevant state agencies, national groups, and educational institutions. Such personnel should be assigned to sub-sections of the Department, such as units of the Public Health Service, Welfare Administration, Social Security Administration, and Vocational Rehabilitation Administration.

A Center on Alcoholism should be established within the National Institute of Mental Health[3]

The federal unit providing leadership for mental health programs and services should also share in assisting problem drinkers. Community mental health programs, which will be the major focus of future mental health activities, present a unique opportunity to improve the care and treatment of problem drinkers.

A Center on Alcoholism within the National Institute of Mental Health would: (1) coordinate the work of the Institute on problem drinking; (2) assist in developing rules and regulations for community mental health grants so that services for problem drinkers will be included in them; and (3) provide funds to state mental health authorities through formula grants or contracts for demonstration and program support to (a) establish an alcoholism unit

3. The establishment of a National Center for Prevention and Control of Alcoholism was announced by President Johnson on October 20, 1966.

(function to be defined in state plans) within state mental health authorities; (b) establish and strengthen alcoholism programs in mental hospitals; and (c) establish and strengthen alcoholism programs within community mental health centers. Such a Center would also: (4) provide funds[4] through formula grants or contracts for demonstration and program support to such agencies as public-welfare and public-health departments, vocational rehabilitation agencies, and state alcoholism programs (when under separate boards or commissions)[5]; (5) conduct and support research on alcohol problems; (6) provide financial assistance to train research and treatment personnel for work in this field; and (7) stimulate interest in alcohol problems among various professional and scientific groups.

Funds should be provided to states and communities for planning activities

State and local activities should be planned so as to maximize the use of existing resources and develop the most appropriate new and expanded programs. Grants-in-aid

4. Arrangements for the granting of such funds should be developed jointly by the Alcoholism Center and other appropriate divisions within the Department of Health, Education, and Welfare.

5. State alcoholism programs have provided substantial leadership at the state level during the last fifteen years. Their particular strength often has been in areas of public and professional education, consultation, and coordination. Such activities are still badly needed and should be greatly expanded; however, it does not appear likely (or desirable) that the bulk of services for problem drinkers will be provided through these specialized programs. As indicated elsewhere in this report, such services will be provided primarily through existing general agencies—mental health, public-health, medical care, public-welfare, and vocational rehabilitation. Nevertheless, grants could be made available to state programs to increase their effectiveness as catalysts and planners, and to enable them to continue in their leadership roles.

(on a formula basis) should be made by the Department of Health, Education, and Welfare to assist states in this work.

Plans to improve treatment services should be part of comprehensive general health and welfare planning at state and local levels. The grants should be used to augment staff so that skilled personnel would be available to deal specifically with questions of services to problem drinkers. In addition, they should be used for setting up collaborative apparatus among state agencies such as liquor control boards (and alcohol tax units), highway departments, motor vehicle administrators, and state departments of education, all of which need to be included in a comprehensive approach. Guidelines for the planning grants would be established by the Intradepartmental Committee and its staff in order to ensure, for example, that each state alcoholism authority (designated by the governor) actively involves relevant state and local agencies and citizens' groups in the planning process. Only after the state plans have been approved by the federal government should program support be made available.

Law enforcement, education, and liquor control are some activities related to alcohol problems that remain primarily the responsibility of state and local governments. Agencies in these fields, individually as well as collaboratively, will need to exercise leadership and develop policies and programs for reducing alcohol problems. Experimentation with various approaches suited to the particular characteristics and needs of different states and communities should be encouraged. No suggestions are being made for a blueprint or detailed plan to be applied throughout the country.

Nevertheless, each state must devise the means for

bringing together—on a regular basis—key personnel from various state agencies whose work relates to alcohol problems; they can develop the type of overall policy most suited to the needs of the particular state. Possibly the agencies involved should be formally designated as the Governor's Committee on Alcohol Problems. Because this type of collaboration has not been previously attempted, state governors may need to give special attention to these efforts in the initial years—this could include the assignment of at least one full-time employee to assist in the planning. It is unlikely that in the absence of deliberate action by the executive branch of state governments the complex and difficult task of developing adequate state plans and policies for the range of alcohol problems can be accomplished.

Active steps are also required to make the best use of the many different community agencies and services that provide treatment to problem drinkers, and to promote continuity of care. Locally, a health department, a mental health center, a health and welfare planning council, or a council on alcoholism could provide such coordination. Personnel with experience in treatment and community organization should be assigned to this work. Unless some staff time is regularly set aside for coordinating activities, the desired results will probably not be achieved.

The planning and coordination of health and welfare services are likely to receive increasing attention in future years. New planning bodies will probably be set up at state levels with authority to develop comprehensive plans that will serve as the basis for the granting of federal funds. Steps should be taken to guarantee that attention is given to the treatment needs of problem drinkers in such planning activities, for there is some danger that emphasis on generalized (non-categorical) health planning may lead to neglect of certain problem areas, particularly where some stigma is associated with the condition.

State and local agencies should assign special personnel to work with problem drinkers

The work of state and local agencies with problem drinkers would be greatly strengthened if they hired special personnel (1) to function as consultants; (2) to assist in the development of special programs for clients of their agency who are problem drinkers; (3) to provide liaison with other agencies; and (4) to ensure that problem drinking is not neglected in the day-to-day activities of their own agency. Such personnel could devote some time also to the direct provision of help to problem drinkers.

Public-health departments, public-welfare agencies, vocational rehabilitation agencies, and correctional departments (parole, probation, and prisons) are major governmental units that currently are in contact with very large numbers of problem drinkers. Expanding their work with these patients would be a most significant step toward strengthening the care and treatment of problem drinkers.

While state and local *mental health agencies* are key providers of care for the emotionally ill and others with psycho-social problems, they have not as a rule assumed leadership in the provision of care for problem drinkers. Therefore, specific budgetary and organizational mechanisms should be provided to ensure that these patients will receive adequate care from mental health agencies. Such steps might include the temporary establishment of alcoholism sections in state mental health departments until responsibility for the care and treatment of problem drinkers could be accepted by general mental health agencies. Funds of the state alcoholism units could function as "seed" money to assist in setting up these special units or programs in mental hospitals. In addition, various safeguards and incentives could be established by the state mental health authorities in their granting of funds to local programs and units to ensure appropriate attention to the needs of problem drinkers.

Local psychiatric services, including *community mental health centers,* should have some personnel (although not necessarily on a full-time basis) who are designated as alcoholism specialists. These staff members would function both in direct service and in consultative capacities. State and local mental health funds also could be used to provide some financial support for transitional facilities such as half-way houses.

The traditional "catalyst" function of *public-health agencies* should be extended to include the area of problem drinking. State and local public-health agencies can and should take on the responsibility of seeing that communities have needed treatment services. In areas lacking strong community mental health programs, health departments can provide leadership in the coordination of treatment services for problem drinkers.

3

The role of non-governmental organizations

While only a few voluntary, non-governmental organizations focus exclusively on problem drinking or other alcohol problems, a large number of such groups do work with alcohol problems. A satisfactory approach to the total range of alcohol problems would mean that many organizations work together and with governmental agencies in an entirely different fashion than in the past. As the climate of emotionalism and controversy surrounding alcohol use and problem drinking gradually changes, cooperation between various groups will be greatly facilitated and it will, in turn, help create a new, less emotionally charged atmosphere. Concerted efforts by non-governmental groups will serve as a major stimulus to greater action by various levels of government. Furthermore, these numerous voluntary organizations command the respect and loyalty of large groups of persons and, in some instances, of key government agencies and officials. Thus, their participation and support are essential to the development and implementation of a total national alcohol policy.

Historically, when the needs of particular persons have

been disregarded, citizens' groups have arisen to call attention to the unmet needs. Such groups then become spokesmen who seek to bring about public education and governmental action. Although deeply engrained cultural attitudes have slowed the development of effective programs for problem drinkers, two voluntary organizations have been of particular importance in this field. They are Alcoholics Anonymous and the National Council on Alcoholism. While A.A. is a loosely knit organization made up of problem drinkers who have joined together in their community, the National Council (NCA) is a national voluntary health organization with numerous affiliates throughout the United States. It was organized in 1944 to "combat alcoholism through a national program of education, research, and community services."

The North American Association of Alcoholism Programs (NAAAP) is composed of administrators of government-supported programs for treatment, education, and research in alcoholism. It was organized late in 1949 as a result of discussions held at the Yale Summer School of Alcohol Studies. Currently over thirty-five states and six Canadian provinces operate special alcoholism programs. In recent years the Association has allowed individuals to join and participate in its activities. In 1963 the NAAAP established a full-time central office in Washington, D.C. The following major activities of this organization are conducted mainly through this office: (1) an annual four-day meeting; (2) interchange of information among member organizations and with other agencies; (3) provision of information about alcoholism and alcoholism programs to members of the federal government, the legislative branch as well as the executive; and (4) organization of conferences and institutes. The Association is taking major responsibility for the planning and organization of the 1968 International Congress on Alcoholism.

The National Council of Alcoholism has played an important role in public education on alcoholism and has been influential in generating support for many governmental alcoholism programs. The major current activities of the Council and its local affiliates are: (1) offering public and professional education on alcoholism aimed at reducing the stigma attached to the condition; (2) providing information and referral services at the community level to problem drinkers and their families and, in some instances, providing short-term counseling, often of an essentially "pre-treatment" nature; and (3) acting as the conscience of the community in relation to alcoholism, by trying to overcome the neglect and to stimulate the development of better services for people with drinking problems.

The National Council on Alcoholism and its affiliates are confronted with some unique opportunities and problems because of the existence of Alcoholics Anonymous. On the one hand, members of A.A. are often significantly involved in the local councils—both at board and staff levels. They represent a very large group of potential volunteers. On the other hand, this is the only health area where such a major mutual aid group exists in addition to the voluntary national and local organizations. Usually there is excellent cooperation between A.A. members and alcoholism councils; however, there is also some competition between the groups. Difficult tasks confronting the N.C.A. are to clarify its identity and to distinguish its goals and methods of operation from those of A.A.

While the number of local councils or committees on alcoholism has grown from 56 to 75 in the last ten years, the voluntary health movement in alcoholism is still small compared to that in mental health, which has close to 800 local chapters. In recent years, the National Association for Mental Health has raised close to $6 million a year, while the figure for the N.C.A. is about $500,000. Founded in 1944, the N.C.A., of course, is much newer—the first mental health association was formed in 1909, the National Tuberculosis Association in 1904, the National Cancer Society in 1913, and the National Foundation (polio) in 1938. In addition, problem drinking is more likely to be stigmatized than heart disease, cancer, or even mental illness; thus the resistance and barriers faced by the alcoholism movement have been far greater. A major source of financial support for the N.C.A. has been one of the few foundations making grants in the field of alcoholism—the Christopher D. Smithers Foundation, established in 1952. In the last ten years it has awarded close to $2 million for projects related to alcoholism; approximately half this amount has been granted to the N.C.A. and its affiliates.

The Yale Center of Alcohol Studies, now at Rutgers, set up as a distinct unit in 1940, has had substantial influence on many developments in the field during the last quarter of a century. In addition to continuing research, documentation, and publication activities, the Rutgers Center is best known for its Summer School of Alcohol Studies. Out of this school have developed numerous other schools and summer institutes throughout the United States and Canada. The Center, through its staff and its summer school, has played a major role in the development of the National Council on Alcoholism, as well as in the organization of many state alcoholism programs (currently most of these programs are directed by people who attended one of the Yale-Rutgers summer training sessions), and in the establishment of models for alcoholism clinics and industrial alcoholism programs. The Center also publishes the only American journal specializing in alcohol problems, the *Quarterly Journal of Studies on Alcohol,* and supports extensive bibliographic and documentation services for scientists, scholars, and practitioners. The Rutgers Center of Alcohol Studies is in a position to contribute significantly toward the study, development, and implementation of a total national alcohol policy.

Until repeal of the Prohibition Amendment the major groups in the United States dealing with alcohol problems were various temperance organizations. A number of these are still active and should be drawn into new efforts to approach alcohol problems. The largest such group is the Women's Christian Temperance Union with 200,000 members; another is the American Council on Alcohol Problems. The American Businessmen's Research Foundation restricts its activities mainly to the publication of statistical information. Allied Youth is a national organization of high school students that promotes "alcohol-free" recreational activities. Active only in certain areas of the country, it has fewer than 20,000 members.

Various church groups have been closely linked to the Temperance Movement. In recent years some have shifted somewhat to concentrating on their own alcohol-education activities. While a number retain emphasis on total abstinence, others have begun to stress moderation and protection against abuse. Many church groups have actively sought to develop more sympathetic attitudes toward problem drinkers. The North Conway (N.H.) Foundation is an interdenominational organization seeking to stimulate church action on alcoholism and related problems. It does not identify itself with a "wet" or "dry" position, although in recent years it has moved toward a discussion of drink-

ing which is somewhat removed from traditional abstinence views. Specialized groups, such as the North Conway Foundation and the Division of Alcohol Problems
and General Welfare within the Methodist Church, interdenominational groups like the National Council of
Churches, individual denominations, and religious leaders
will all need to be drawn into discussions about acceptable
and unacceptable drinking and the related issues of alcohol
education.

While most temperance groups have been active in
school education, only one national organization has
sought to approach these problems without taking an explicit position on the "wet-dry" issue. This is the Association for the Advancement of Instruction about Alcohol
and Narcotics. An outgrowth of the Yale-Rutgers Center,
its members consist primarily of teachers and health educators who seek to develop better instruction about alcohol. The major activities of the Association have been
providing for the exchange of information among its small
group of members, and publishing a professional journal.
There are numerous large and powerful groups within the
field of education that should be involved in efforts to develop a radically different and improved climate for alcohol education in the schools. Such organizations are the
National Education Association (NEA), National Congress of Parents and Teachers (PTA's), American Feder-
ation of Teachers, National Association of School Boards,
American Association of School Administrators, Society of
Public Health Educators, and the Association of Colleges
and Secondary Schools.

The bulk of the treatment and rehabilitation of problem
drinkers will probably be provided by basic American
"helping agencies." The associations to which the staff of

these agencies belong can all assist significantly by encouraging greater interest among their members in overcoming the neglect of problem drinkers. These associations include the American Medical Association, American Psychiatric Association, American Public Health Association, American Psychological Association, National Association of Social Workers, American Hospital Association, Family Service Association of America, American Rehabilitation Association, American Correctional Association, National League of Nursing, and the American Public Welfare Association. Each of these groups holds regular meetings and maintains a full-time staff in its national office. Their participation is essential if treatment services are to be improved. In addition, the National Association for Mental Health—the major voluntary organization in the mental health field—could work collaboratively with the National Council on Alcoholism in strengthening the latter's efforts at citizen education and organization of services for problem drinkers.

Special mention must be made of the Salvation Army and the Volunteers of America, both of which have long provided substantial amounts of care for men and women in the Skid Row sections of large American cities. While the Salvation Army has a primarily religious and evangelical emphasis, in recent years more of its centers have been employing professionally trained personnel, particularly social workers. The Salvation Army often provides care and shelter for homeless men and women when local welfare agencies do not offer such assistance.

A major thesis of this report is the importance of the relationship between "normal" drinking patterns and the nature and extent of problem drinking. In the section on the prevention of problem drinking, proposals that American drinking patterns be modified have been made. It has been suggested that both the alcoholic beverage industry and various state liquor control authorities might participate in bringing about changes in drinking patterns. The three major groups representing the industry are the Wine Institute, U.S. Brewers' Association, and Licensed Beverage Industries, Inc. (L.B.I.). In recent years both the Brewers' Association and the L.B.I. have made small grants for research on problem drinking and other alcohol problems. In addition, the L.B.I. has supported some projects aimed at improving alcohol education in the schools. The specific manner in which the alcoholic beverage industry will join in a national effort remains to be worked out, however.

Each of the fifty states has an alcoholic beverage authority. In some states the authority is a separate agency, while in others it is a unit in a larger department. In seventeen states, generally referred to as "monopoly" or "control" states, liquor is sold only through state-owned stores. The organization of these seventeen liquor control boards is the National Alcoholic Beverage Control Association. Their counterpart for the "free" or "license" states is the Conference of State Liquor Administrators. Both groups are, of course, deeply involved in rules and regulations regarding the distribution and sale of beverage alcohol and, in the "control" states, in the direct sale of alcoholic beverages to the public. It is remarkable that their activities have been almost totally isolated from those of others concerned with alcohol problems.

American law-enforcement agencies, courts, and penal institutions are abundantly aware of the impact of alcohol on their day-to-day work—because of the massive number of arrests for public drunkenness and the frequently reported link between alcohol and crime. Specialists in the traffic field, such as the National Safety Council, the American Automobile Association, the American Association of Motor Vehicle Adminstrators, the Association of Driver Education Instructors, and the casualty insurance companies, should work with educators, clergymen, social scientists, health workers, the alcoholic beverage industry, and state liquor control authorities in bringing about changes in American drinking patterns.

A number of organizations of government officials are in a position to exert great influence on the development of a national alcohol policy and program. These organizations have full-time staffs and hold annual meetings at which issues about alcohol policy could be discussed constructively. Their meetings also provide a national forum for officials from state and local levels of government. Key groups in this category are the Council of State Governments, which publishes widely distributed reports and is responsible for the annual Governors' Conference; the U. S. Mayors' Conferences; the National League of Cities; and the International Association of City Managers. The officials represented by such groups should participate in efforts to cope more effectively with alcohol problems.

Finally, there are unique opportunities for the large foundations to aid the development of a new American alcohol policy. Foundations have a freedom and flexibility not available to government, which is particularly essential in fields where innovation and experimentation are required, and where new types of solutions are needed. Leadership by foundations could be unusually fruitful.

The enormous complexity of American society is amply demonstrated by the listing above of some of the groups that should be actively involved in one way or another in a comprehensive approach to alcohol problems. Also shown is the extent to which alcohol problems and issues penetrate contemporary American life. The diversity of interests and points of view is also abundantly clear, and developing consensus in areas where agreement is possible will not be an easy task or soon achieved. Yet cooperation is immediately feasible in many areas and should become more extensive as progress is made in creating an atmosphere for discussion of and action on alcohol problems.

The Commission proposes the formulation of a national public policy on alcohol and it believes that such a comprehensive policy can be developed. The Commission recommends that an integrated conceptual approach be substituted for the current patchwork of actions. The extent and character of the proposed changes should not be underestimated. A thorough examination is needed of individual and group behavior. It should now be possible for professional workers and the American people generally to look at drinking patterns to examine their strengths and weaknesses, and to move toward modifying types of drinking that are damaging and unacceptable. The Commission believes that there is substantial, if not conclusive, evidence that such modifications will reduce rates of alcoholism and other types of problem drinking.

These are sweeping proposals for broad social changes. Their scope is great and their demands severe. They ask that the public assume total responsibility for alcohol; that the painful and troubled experiences of Prohibition be put aside; and that current social freedoms surrounding alcohol use be critically examined and scientifically studied for their strengths and weaknesses. A major shift in social attitudes and policies is required to match the prevalence, the persistency, the complexity, and the interrelatedness of alcohol problems.

Appendix A

The American Medical Association Statement on Alcoholism by the House of Delegates, American Medical Association (November 1956).

Alcoholic symptomatology and complications which occur in many personality disorders come within the scope of medical practice.

Acute alcoholic intoxication can be and often is a medical emergency. As with any other acute case, the merits of each individual case should be considered at the time of the emergency.

The type of alcoholic patient admitted to a general hospital should be judged on his individual merits, consideration being given to the attending physician's opinion, cooperation of the patient, and his behavior at the time of admission. The admitting doctors should then examine the patient and determine from the history and his actions whether he should be admitted or refused.

In order to offer house officers well-rounded training in the general hospital, there should be adequate facilities available as part of a hospital program for care of alcoholics. Since the house officer in a hospital will eventually come in contact with this type of patient in practice, his training in treating this illness should come while he is a resident officer. Hospital staffs should be urged to accept these patients for treatment and cooperate in this program.

With improved means of treatment available and the changed viewpoint and attitude which places the alcoholic in the category of a sick individual, most of the problems formerly encountered in the treatment of the alcoholic in a general hospital have been greatly reduced. In any event, the individual patient should be evaluated rather than have general objection on the grounds of a diagnosis of alcoholism.

It is recognized that no general policy can be made for all hospitals. Administrators are urged to give careful consideration to the possibility of accepting such patients in the light of the newer available measures and the need for providing facilities for treating these patients. In order to render a service to the community, provision should be made for such patients who cooperate and who wish such care.

In order to accomplish any degree of success with the problem of alcoholism, it is necessary that educational programs be enlarged, methods of case findings and follow-up be ascertained, research be encouraged, and general education toward acceptance of these sick people be emphasized. The hospital and its administration occupy a unique position in the community which allows them great opportunities to contribute to the accomplishment of this purpose. It is urged that general hospitals and their administrators and staffs give thought to meeting this responsibility.

Appendix B

American Hospital Association Statement on Alcoholism and the General Hospital (September 1957).

Alcoholism is a serious health problem. It falls within the scope of medical practice and it is often a medical emergency.

The alcoholic should not be denied the advantage of a thorough study of the cause or causes of his condition and should not be denied the advantage of the best possible management of his case.

In 1944, a special committee of the American Hospital Association recommended that *"the primary point of attack (on alcoholism) should be through the general hospital. Because of the completeness of its facilities and of its accessibility, it is the logical place to which an alcoholic or his family would turn."*

There are still many hospitals that deny admission to all alcoholic patients despite the availability of improved methods of treatment and demonstration by experience that only a minority of patients with acute alcoholism are uncooperative.

Such a policy denies to the alcoholic patient benefits which would be available to him were his acute poisoning from another source, such as food, etc. It also denies to hospital attendants and house staffs opportunities for education in the management of the alcoholic patient.

The American Hospital Association urges general hospitals to develop a program for the care of alcoholics and, having done so, to base the decision as to admission or nonadmission of the patient with a diagnosis of alcoholism upon the condition and needs of the individual patient.

This progressive step would keep pace with increased recognition of (1) the general hospital as the community health center, and (2) alcoholism as a medical problem requiring broad-scale attack if it is to be solved.

Appendix C

Position Statement of the American Psychiatric Association Concerning Responsibility of Psychiatrists and Other Physicians for Alcohol Problems (February 1965).

An adequate national attack on alcohol problems* necessarily requires the application of the knowledge of many professionals reinforced by broad citizen support. Psychiatrists, together with general physicians and other medical specialists, have a continuing obligation and responsibility for contributing their relevant clinical knowledge and skills to the treatment and prevention of alcohol problems. It is urgent and imperative that psychiatrists and other physicians better prepare themselves for their proper role in attacking these problems on a national scale so that the medical contribution may become far more telling than it has been in the past.

Existing programs in the community for the management of alcohol problems are generally inadequate and need expansion and acceleration. General medical and

---

* The term "alcohol problems" is used advisedly in preference to the term "alcoholic" and "alcoholism" which, in our view are stereotyping and over-simplifying, suggesting that all persons with alcohol problems suffer from the same affliction. They do not, except in the sense that drinking alcohol is contraindicated for them.

psychiatric facilities, including general hospitals and psychiatric facilities, commonly discriminate against the patient with alcohol problems. Such meager services as they do render are offered in a spirit of therapeutic pessimism. What is needed are properly equipped and adequately staffed wards prepared to offer prompt and adequate treatment of acute and chronic physiological, psychological and social disturbances associated with alcohol problems, and all of this in close collaborative relationship with other community agencies concerned with the management of such problems. The principle of a continuum of services in the community applies here as well as to other kinds of disorders.

All prepayment plans for defraying the cost of medical care through insurance should cover the person presenting symptoms of alcohol problems who seeks treatment in medical settings on the same basis as for other illnesses.

Medically speaking, every person with alcohol problems should have the benefit of comprehensive diagnostic study including an assessment of his general health, his mental and emotional condition, and his social and economic adjustments. To concentrate exclusively on "the drinking problem" *per se* is to neglect the possibility of related diseases and various social and economic factors of possible critical import.

Treatment should reflect closely the results of careful diagnostic evaluation. As treatment progresses, furthermore, therapists should maintain continuous surveillance of the effects of that treatment and of intercurrent changes in the patient's condition. Critical review should continuously determine whether treatment is effective, appropriate and adequate.

The patient and his problems with alcohol are affected

by his social environment but they also affect that environment. Treatment programs should take this into account. Persons whose training is other than medical or psychiatric contribute substantially to the understanding and management of the patient. The treating physician should be willing to consult and collaborate with nonmedical individuals and institutions involved without assuming administrative or other nonmedical responsibilities in doing so. Such individuals include clinical psychologists, social workers, nurses, clergymen, vocational rehabilitation counselors, policemen, and others with qualifying education and background. Especially helpful with selected patients are organizations such as Alcoholics Anonymous. When collaborating or consulting with nonmedical persons and organizations, the physician will of course be always mindful of his medical obligations to his patient. He has neither legal nor moral authority to abandon those obligations.

Present research activities investigating the nature and causes of alcohol problems are both commendable and productive. They have not yet, however, reached levels commensurate with the magnitude of the alcohol problem and its threat to our society. Urgently needed are greatly increased public and private monies for research, expanded research institutes and programs, and large numbers of fully-trained personnel to conduct those institutes and programs. Procedures should also be developed which will greatly accelerate the adaption of research findings to the problems of patients and their promulgation to personnel involved.

We urge members of the Association to work with others in their communities for more adequate services for patients with alcohol problems in the context of this statement. We record our conviction of the need for undergraduate and graduate medical educators in general, and psychiatric educators in particular, to orient medical students in these constructive directions.

Appendix D

Research Staff of the Cooperative Commission on the Study of Alcoholism

SENIOR STAFF

Christian Bay Ph.D., L.L.B.	1961-1966
Howard Becker# Ph.D.	1962-1964
Eva Blum Ph.D.	1962-1964
Sidney Cahn	1963-1966
Mervin Freedman# Ph.D.	1962-1964
E. M. Jellinek Sc.D.	1962-1963
Mary Jones# Ph.D.	1961-1965
Joseph Katz# Ph.D.	1961-1964
Max M. Levin Ph.D.	1961-1966
William Madsen Ph.D.	1963-1964
Thomas Plaut Ph.D., M.P.H.	1963-1966
Nevitt Sanford Ph.D.	1961-1966

(#—Part-Time)

CONSULTANTS AND RESEARCH ASSISTANTS

Barry Berkman L.L.B.	1963-1964
Ira Deitrick L.L.B.	1962-1963
Joan Grusec Ph.D.	1962-1963
John Howard Ph.D.	1963-1964
Peter Janke	1963
Lauren Klein	1963-1964

Patricia Kollings M.A.	1962-1966
Magorah Marayama Ph.D.	1962-1964
Anne Miner	1963-1964
Bernard Riback	1964
Robert Russell Ph.D.	1962
Henry Selby Ph.D.	1961-1964
Fred Strassburger Ph.D.	1961-1963
Paul Verden Ph.D.	1962-1965
Rupert Wilkinson	1962-1966